Jeremiah
A Drama in Nine Scenes

by Stefan Zweig

Translated
from the Author's revised German Text
by
Eden and Cedar Paul

Libology Publishing
Lewis Center, Ohio
United States of America

Libology Publishing, 2012.

ISBN-13: 978-0615628899
ISBN-10: 0615628893

Table of Contents

Scene   Page

I   The Awakening of the Prophet   1
II   The Warning   19
III   Rumors   49
IV   The Watch on the Ramparts   67
V   The Prophet's Ordeal   95
VI   Voices in the Night   121
VII   The Supreme Affliction   163
VIII   The Conversion   183
IX   The Everlasting Road   215

to
FRIEDERIKE MARIA von WINTERNITZ

Easter 1915–Easter 1917

THE AWAKENING OF THE PROPHET

THE PERSONS OF THE DRAMA

Zedekiah, the King.
Pashur, the High Priest.
Nahum, the Steward.
Imre, the oldest Burgher.
Abimelech, the General.
Hananiah, the Prophet of the People.
Swordbearers, Warriors.

Jeremiah.
His Mother.
Jochebed, a Relative.
Ahab, the Servingman.
Baruch, a young Man.
Zebulon, his Father.

The People of Jerusalem.
The Envoys of Nebuchadnezzar.
Chaldean and Egyptian Warriors.

The action takes place in Jerusalem at the time of the Destruction of the City.

SCENE ONE

Call unto me, and I will answer thee, and show thee great and mighty things, which thou knowest not. Jeremiah XXXIII, 3.

SCENE ONE

The flat roof of Jeremiah's house; the white flagstones gleam in the dim moonlight. Below are seen the towers and battlements of sleeping Jerusalem. Nothing stirs, save that from time to time we hear the whispering of the breeze that heralds the dawn.

Of a sudden, impetuous footsteps sound upon the stair. Jeremiah staggers in; his robe is torn open at the throat; he gasps like one being strangled.

Jeremiah
They batter in the gates ... to the walls ... to the walls!... Faithless watchmen ... they are coming ... they are upon us.... The temple is in flames.... Help, help!... The walls are breached.... [He has rushed forward to the edge of the roof, where he abruptly stops. His cry rends the shimmering silence. With a start, he awakens from his trance. He looks forth over the town like a drunken man; his arms, which in his terror he has raised, sink slowly to his sides; then wearily he draws his hand across his open eyes] Illusion! Once again these terrible visions. Full, how full, is the House of Dreams! [He leans on the parapet and gazes down] Peace broods over the city; the country is at peace; in me alone, in my breast alone, this fire rages. How quietly the town reposes in God's arms, nestling in slumber, roofed over by peace, the moonbeams falling on every house, and every house plunged in gentle sleep. But I, I alone, am consumed with fire night after night; I crash earthward with the falling towers, rush to escape, perish amid the flames; I, and none but I, my bowels troubled, leap heated from my bed and stagger forth into the moonlight seeking coolness! For me alone comes a vision to shatter sleep; for me alone does a fiery horror wrench the darkness from my lids. The martyrdom of this vision; the madness of these faces which swarm in their blood-stained multitude and then fade in the clear moonlight!

Always the same dream, the same illusion. Night after night, the same terror seizes me, the same dream, culminating in the same torment. Who has instilled this dream poison into my veins? Who hunts me thus with terror? Who covets my sleep, that he must rob me of it; who is my torturer, and for whom must I thus hold vigil? Answer! Who art thou, invisible one, aiming at me from the darkness thy wingèd shafts? Who art thou, terror incarnate, coming to lie with me by night, quickening me with thy spirit until my frame is twisted as with labor pains? Wherefore in this slumbering city should the curse be laid on me alone? [He is silent, straining his ear to the all-pervading silence, and then continues with growing excitement] Silence, nothing but silence, while within is unceasing turmoil and storm-tossed night. With scorching talons it tears at my vitals and yet cannot grasp them. I am scourged with visions, and know not who holds the scourge. My cries go forth into the void. Desist, invisible hunter, or if it must be otherwise, seize your quarry; call to me when I wake, not when I sleep; speak to me in words, not in visions. Reveal what you are hiding from me; tell me the meaning of these torments.

A Voice

[Calling softly from the darkness. It seems to come from far above or far beneath, mysterious in its remoteness] Jeremiah!

Jeremiah

[Staggers as if struck by a stone] Who calls? Surely I heard my name? Was it a voice from the stars, or was it the voice of my own dream? [He listens. All is quiet again] Is it thou, invisible one, who huntest me and tormentest me? Or is it I myself; is it the fierce current of my own blood? Voice, speak once more, that I may know thee. Call to me once again.

The Voice

[Drawing nearer] Jeremiah!

Jeremiah

[Quailing, sinks to his knees] Here am I, Lord! Thy servant heareth. [Breathless he hearkens. Nothing stirs; he trembles with emotion] Speak, Lord, to thy servant. Thou didst call my name. Give me thy message that I may understand it. I am ready for thy word and await thy command. [He listens again with strained attention. Profound silence] Is it presumption that I should long for thee? I am no more than an ignorant fellow, a man of no account, a speck of dust in the world thou hast made, but thine is all power of choice. Thou who choosest kings from among shepherds, and who often unsealest the lips of a boy so that he glows with thy speech, thy choice is made by other tokens. Whom thou touchest, Lord, he is chosen; whom thou choosest, Lord, he is appointed.

If it were thy call which came to me, lo I have hearkened to the call. If it be thou, Lord, who huntest me, I flee thee not. Seize thy quarry, Lord, seize thy prey; or hunt me yet farther to the goal! But make thyself known, that I may not fail thee; reveal the heaven of thy word, that I, thy servant, may behold thee!

The Voice
[Nearer and more urgent] Jeremiah!

Jeremiah
[Rapturously] I hear, Lord, I hear. With all my soul I listen to thy word. Unworthy vessel that I am, I wait to be filled with thy message. I vow myself to thy service, Lord, to thine alone, for my soul is athirst to serve thee. I await thy word and thy sign.

The Voice of Jeremiah's Mother
[Now close at hand and plainly recognizable] Jeremiah!

Jeremiah
[In ecstasy] Show thyself to me, Lord; my heart is racked with the imminence of thy coming. Pour forth thy waters, holy storm; plough me up, that I may bear thy seed; make my earth fruitful, inspire my lips; brand me with the mark of thy service! Set thy yoke upon me. See, my neck is bowed in readiness, for thine am I, thine for evermore. Make thyself known to me, Lord, even as I know thee; let me but see thy glory, even as thou lookest down upon my unworthiness in the gloom; deign only to show me the way of thy will, point the way to him who is thy servant for ever!

The Mother
[Her search has led her up the stair; her countenance shows anxiety, her voice is full of tenderness] Here at last I find you, my son.

Jeremiah
[Springing to his feet in fear and wrath] Begone! Alas the voices are stilled; the way is lost, never shall I find it again.

6

The Mother

Woe is me, why do you stand here so thinly clad in the chill night air?
Come down, my son. The morning mist brings fever.

Jeremiah

[Wildly] Why do you follow me, why do you pester me? Unending chase.
You follow me without pause, waking or sleeping.

The Mother

Jeremiah, what do you mean? I was sleeping below, and then I seemed to
hear people talking on the roof.

Jeremiah

You heard, you too? God's holy truth! You heard him speak? Understood
his call?

The Mother

Whom do you mean? You have no companion.

Jeremiah

[Seizing her arm] Mother, tell me I beseech you. Death or joy hangs upon
your words. Did you hear a voice; did you hear it after you had
awakened?

The Mother

I heard a voice on the roof and went to summon you. But your bed was
cold and empty. Then fear came upon me, and I called your name.

Jeremiah

[Trembling] You called my name?

The Mother

Thrice did I call you. But why ...

Jeremiah

Thrice? Mother, are you certain ...

The Mother

Thrice did I call you.

Jeremiah

[His voice breaking] Disaster and derision! Fraud everywhere, without and within. There came an earnest call, and in my terror I thought it was God.

The Mother

How strange you are! I meant no harm. Since there was no answer, I came to the roof to see if there was anyone here. I found no one.

Jeremiah

Nay, you found a madman. The torture of these visions! Sense and nonsense join in cheating me. I am befooled by my own fantasy.

The Mother

What are you talking about? What is troubling you?

Jeremiah

Nothing, Mother, nothing. Pay no heed to my words.

The Mother

I must heed them, Jeremiah; but they are dark to me. An evil mood has beset you, and has estranged you from me. What has happened; what is tormenting you?

Jeremiah

Nothing is tormenting me, Mother. I was too hot in bed, and sought the roof for coolness.

The Mother

You are closing your heart to me, and yet I can read you. I know that night after night for months past you have been wandering about. I have often heard you groaning in your sleep. When you have left your bed to walk restlessly in the darkness, my heart has followed your every step. Tell me your troubles. Shut not yourself away from me.

Jeremiah
Do not concern yourself about it, Mother.

The Mother
How can I help but concern myself about it? Are you not the day of my days and the prayer of my nights? You have outgrown the arms which used to carry you; but I still hold you in my soul, which watches over your life. I knew, ere you yourself were aware; I saw months ago, before you yourself had seen. I saw the shadow upon your brow and the anguish of your soul. You have become a stranger to your friends; you shun merrymakings; you keep away from the marketplace and from the dwellings of men. Buried in thought, you renounce life. Jeremiah, bethink yourself. You were trained for the priesthood. Your father's mantle awaits you, that you may praise the Lord with psaltery and song. Look forth from the darkness into the daylight. The hour has come for you to begin your life's work.

Jeremiah
Not now the time for beginnings. The end draws nigh.

The Mother
It is time! It is time! Long since have you grown to manhood. The house has need of a wife, and of children to raise up seed to your father.

Jeremiah
[In bitter distress] Lead a wife home to desolation? Beget children for the slaughter? In sooth, it is not the bridal hour that approaches!

The Mother
I do not understand.

Jeremiah
Shall I build a house in the abyss? Shall I build my life in death? Shall I sow corruption, and sing the praises of disaster? I say unto you, Mother,

blessed is he whose heart is now free from ties to the living, for whosoever breathes this day is already drinking the waters of death.

The Mother
What mad fancy has seized you? When were the times more propitious? When was the land more peaceful?

Jeremiah
No, Mother, the fools say: Peace, Peace. But their words do not bring peace. They lie down to sleep unheeding, and as they sleep they are on their way to death. A time is coming such as Israel has never yet known, a war such as the world has never yet seen. The living will covet the peace of the dead in their graves, and those who can see will envy the darkness with which the blind are stricken. Not yet can the fools see, not yet is it manifest to the dreamers; but I have beheld it night after night. Higher leap the flames, nearer comes the foe; the day of tumult and destruction is at hand; war's red star is rising on the night.

The Mother
[Greatly moved] How know you these things?

Jeremiah
A word has come to me in secret,
For I have seen faces in the night,
I have wandered in my dreams.
Fear and dread fell upon me,
I trembled in every limb,
And like a crumbling wall
My heart fainted within me.
Mother,
Such sights have I seen,
That, if they were written,
Men's hair would stand on end,
And sleep would depart from them
For ever.

The Mother

Jeremiah, what do you mean?

Jeremiah

The end draweth near; the end!
Evil appeareth out of the north,
Fire is its chariot,
Massacre its pinions!
Already the heavens ring with terror,
The earth shakes with the stamping of the hoofs.

The Mother

[Horrified] Jeremiah!

Jeremiah

[Seizing her arm, listens] Do you hear, do you not hear, the rushing of chariots?

The Mother

I hear nothing! Day is dawning. The shepherds are piping in the valleys, and a gentle breeze blows across the roof.

Jeremiah

A gentle breeze?
Woe is me!
With mighty roaring
The wind is rising,
The whirlwind of God.
From the caverns
Of the north down-rushing,
Terror it brandishes
Over the town.
Mother! Mother! Do you not hear it?
Swords clash in the wind,
Loud roar the chariot wheels,
The night flashes with lances and with armor;
Warrior upon warrior, countless in number,

11

The whirlwind scatters over the land.

The Mother
All is illusion, the madness of dreams!

Jeremiah
They are coming, they are coming,
Strangers from the east,
Men of an ancient people,
Men of a mighty people.
They hasten from the east
In unending files;
Their arrows speed like lightning;
Their chargers are shod with swiftness;
Their chariots are solid as rock.
Among them there rideth,
With blood-stained crown,
The destroyer of cities
By fire and sword,
The tyrant of nations,
The king of kings from the north.

The Mother
The king from the north? You dream. The king from the north!

Jeremiah
Whom the Lord has awakened
That he may scourge the people for all its transgressions,
That he may crumble the walls and throw down the towers,
That he may quench the light and the laughter of homes,
That he may raze the city and the temple to the ground,
And that he may plough up the streets of Jerusalem.

The Mother
Blasphemous folly! The city endureth for ever!

Jeremiah
It is falling!
The onslaughts of God
None may withstand!
Below ground
Its roots shall wither,
Above ground
Its fruits shall rot!
With axe and with fire
The horsemen shall ravage
Israel's forest and Zion's fair plains.

The Mother
[Breaking in] It is false!
Ne'er shall an enemy circle our wall,
David's city be taken, Jerusalem fall.
Though foes from the ends of the earth should rage,
The towering battlements ever shall stand.
Firm Israel's heart, and mighty her hand,
Eternal the days of Jerusalem!

Jeremiah
It is falling! Broken is the staff and foretold is the hour. The end draws near, the end of Israel.

The Mother
False prophet! We are the elect of the Lord, and our strength shall endure through the ages! Never shall Jerusalem perish!

Jeremiah
I have seen it in my dreams; 'twas made plain to my eyes.

The Mother
Evil is he who dreams such dreams, and seven times an evildoer he who believes them. Alas that I should have lived to see this day when my own

blood is fearful for Zion and has lost faith in the Lord! Jeremiah, do you wish me to curse the womb that bore you?

Jeremiah
The horror came upon me against my will; naught could I do to ward off the faces.

The Mother
Watch and pray against them and shatter their lies in the name of the Lord. Forget not, Jeremiah, that you are an anointed and consecrated son, that your voice should praise the Lord, that you should uplift the hearts of the sorrowful and fill with hope the minds of the despairing!

Jeremiah
How can I? My own despair is the greatest of all. Leave me, Mother, leave me!

The Mother
I will not leave you, neither will I abandon your soul to despair. Jeremiah, my only son, hearken to me. For the first time let me tell you something which may awaken your courage. Hear the words that are forced from me by my distress. I, too, was once filled with despair, inasmuch as for ten years the Lord had closed my womb. I was the sport of my companions and the mock of the concubines. For ten long years I bore my lot patiently, and had almost given up hope; but in the eleventh year my heart was kindled, and I went to the house of God to implore him that my womb should bear fruit. Throwing myself on the ground, I watered it with tears, vowing that if a son were vouchsafed me I would devote him to the Lord's service. I swore to be silent, to utter no word during my time of trial, that my son in days to come might speak abundantly, praising God.

Jeremiah
You also consecrated me, Mother?

The Mother
The selfsame day your father knew me and I was blessed with you. Hearken, Jeremiah. For nine months did I faithfully refrain from speech

that you might speak abundantly, that you might glorify the everlasting God! Thus did I fulfil my vow, and we brought you up to read the scripture, and sweetly did you sing to the psaltery. Know, then, that from the first you were a consecrated priest and devoted to the service of the Lord. Rend the veil of your dreams and come forth into the daylight.

Jeremiah

A double consecration, Mother, a twofold witness of this night. A second time you have called me to life. Through your words the light has come to me, for, wonderful to relate, I cried my question to God and he sent you to speak to me! Now do I know who knocked on the wall of my sleep until I awakened from my life's slumber; now do I know who summoned me.

The Mother

What has befallen you? Your words are like those of a drunken man.

Jeremiah

Yea, drunk am I now with the certainty of his will; so full am I of speech, that the words must forth. The seals upon my mouth are broken, and my lips burn to utter the revelation.

The Mother

Woe is me if you should reveal your mad dreams. You are no son of mine if you cry such fancies aloud!

Jeremiah

Your son, Mother? Indeed and indeed I am your son, with a fate like unto yours! Learn that I too have been barren, and that the Lord hath quickened me with a word and a secret. I have renewed your vow, Mother, and have given myself to the Lord.

The Mother

Go, then, to God's house. Give yourself to him who has called you, praise his holy name.

Jeremiah

Nay, Mother, not for me the service of the sacrificial priest. I myself must be the sacrifice. For God my veins run blood; for him my flesh is consumed; for him my soul burns. I will serve him as none ever served him before; his paths shall henceforward be mine. Behold the dawn upon the valley, and within me likewise is darkness dispelled by light! God's heaven flames, and in me no less the heart is aflame. Chariot of Elijah, fiery chariot, carry my words that they may fall like thunder into the hearts of men. My lips scorch me, I must go, I must go.

The Mother

Whither would you go ere the day has well begun?

Jeremiah

I know not, God knoweth.

The Mother

Tell me what you mean to do.

Jeremiah

I know not, I know not! My heart is his, and my deeds are his.

The Mother

Jeremiah, you shall not go unless you swear to me to say naught of your dreams ...

Jeremiah

I will not swear! I am vowed to him alone.

The Mother

... to refrain from breathing terror into the people.

Jeremiah

His is the revelation, mine are the lips alone!

The Mother

Woe is me, you will not hearken to my words. Know, then, that he who sows despair in Israel shall never enter my house more.

Jeremiah

His is my word; my dwelling is his care.

The Mother

Who believes not in Zion is no longer my son.

Jeremiah

I am his alone, his who placed me within thy womb.

The Mother

You will go then? But first hear me, Jeremiah, hear me before you open your lips to the people. With all my strength do I curse him who spreads terror over Israel, I curse ...

Jeremiah

[Shuddering] Curse not, Mother, curse not!

The Mother

I curse him who saith the walls shall fall and the streets be laid waste; I curse him who cries death over Israel. May his body be consumed with fire and his soul fall into the hands of the living God.

Jeremiah

Curse not, Mother ...

The Mother

I curse the unbeliever, who has more faith in his own dreams than in God's mercy. Cursèd be he who denies God, were he my own son! For the last time, Jeremiah, choose!

Jeremiah

I follow my own path. [With heavy steps he makes ready to descend the stair]

The Mother

Jeremiah, my only son, the stay of my old age, bring not my curse upon you, for God will hear it as he heard my vow.

Jeremiah

I, too, am vowed to him, Mother; me also has he heard. Farewell! [He descends the first step]

The Mother

[With a loud cry] Jeremiah! You trample me down. Your footsteps crush my heart.

Jeremiah

I know not the road along which I move. All I know is that one calls me, and I follow the call. [He slowly goes down the stair, his face expressing restrained emotion, and his gaze turned heavenward]

The Mother

[Rushing in despair to the top of the staircase] Jeremiah! Jeremiah! Jeremiah!

[There is no answer. Her cry sinks to a wail, and after a while she is silent. Her figure, broken with grief, is silhouetted against the sky, where the colors of dawn are showing in fire and blood]

THE WARNING

SCENE TWO

The prophets that have been before me and before thee of old prophesied both against many countries, and against great kingdoms, of war, and of evil, and of pestilence.

The prophet which prophesieth of peace, when the word of the prophet shall come to pass, then shall the prophet be known, that the Lord hath truly sent him. Jeremiah, XXVIII, 8 and 9.

SCENE TWO

The great square of Jerusalem. Thence a broad long flight of steps leads to the porch of pillars of the fortress of Zion; on the right is the king's palace and in the center the adjoining temple. On the other side the great square is bounded by houses and streets which seem low and mean in contrast with the towering structures facing them. The walls of the entrances to the palace are lined with cedar, carved with figures of cherubim, palm trees, and open flowers, all overlaid with gold; there are lavers in the foreground with running water. In the background are seen the brazen gates of the temple.

In front of the palace, in the streets and on the stairway, the people of Jerusalem move to and fro confusedly; a motley mass of men, women, and children, swayed by strong excitement, and in eager expectation. Many voices rise from the crowd, usually in animated dispute, but uniting at times to a single cry. When the scene opens, all have pressed towards the streets and are restlessly expectant.

Voices
The sentinel has already given the signal from the tower.—No, not yet.—But I heard the trumpet.—So did I.—So did I.—They must be close at hand.—From which side are they coming?—Shall we see them?

Other Voices
They are coming from Moria Gate.—They must pass this way as they go to the palace.—Don't block up the whole street.—We want to get a sight of them.—Stand back.—Room, room for the Egyptians.

A Voice
But is it certain that they are coming?

Another Voice
I myself spoke to the messenger who brought the tidings.

Voices
He spoke with the messenger.—Tell us all about it.—How many are there?—Do they bring gifts?—Who is their leader?—Speak up, Issachar!

20

[A group forms round Issachar]

Issachar

I can only tell you what the messenger, my father-in-law, told me.
Pharaoh is sending the finest warriors of Egypt. With them are many
slaves bearing gifts. Nothing like these gifts has come to Zion since the
days of Solomon.

Voices

Long live Pharaoh!—Glory to his reign!—Hail Egypt!

An Old Man

No alliance with Egypt! Their wars are not ours!

Issachar

But our need is the same as theirs. They do not want to be the slaves of
the Chaldeans.

Voices

Nor we, nor we.—Down with Ashur.—Let us break the yoke.—Let us be on
our guard.

Baruch

[A young man, in great excitement] We spend our days in chains. Month
after month, when the moon is new, our messengers go forth to Babylon
bearing tribute of golden shekels. How long shall we suffer it?

Zebulon

[Baruch's father] Silence. It is not for you to speak. A light yoke is the
yoke of Chaldea.

Voices

But we want no yoke at all.—The day of freedom has dawned.—Down
with Ashur!—Let us form an alliance with the Egyptians.

Zebulon
Never did good come out of Mizraim. We must feel our way cautiously, patient and ever mistrustful.

Voices
We must renew the furniture of the temple.—No longer shall Baal enjoy our holy things.—Down with the robbers of the temple!—Now is the appointed hour.

Other Voices
[From farther up the street] They are coming! They are coming!

Voices
[From all sides] Here they are.—Make room.—Come higher up.—Come back here.—I can see them already. You can see them from here.

[The people swarm up the steps and form a lane through which the Egyptian embassy can pass to the palace. At first nothing can be seen of the newcomers but the spear points showing above the noisy throng]

Voices
How finely they march.—Who is the leader?—Araxes is their leader.—Look at the gifts.—Look at the carrying chairs.—One of them is curtained. —That must be Pharaoh's daughter.—Hail Araxes!—Hail Egypt!—Those are heavy chests; there must be gold in them!—We shall have to pay for it with our blood!—How short their swords are.—Ours are better.—Look at their proud gait.—They must be mighty warriors.—Long live Pharaoh-Necho.—Hail Egypt!—God punish Ashur.—Hail Araxes!—Blessings on Pharaoh!—Blessings on the alliance!

[With frenzied acclamations, the people close in upon the procession of the Egyptians. These latter, richly appareled, march proudly by. They rattle their swords and make gracious acknowledgments]

Baruch
[Speaking from the steps] May the king fulfil your wishes! May he cement the alliance!

[The Egyptians have mounted the steps to the palace, and have entered the porch of pillars. The people throng at their heels. Other sections of the crowd disappear into the streets. On the steps there now remain only isolated groups of the older men, while the soldiers and the women hasten after the Egyptians, eager to see what they are bearing, and vanishing after the train in the entry to the palace]

Baruch
[Who has been looking on in ecstasy] I must go with them.

Zebulon
Stay where you are.

Baruch
I want to see for myself how Israel rises against the oppressors. My soul is consumed with desire to behold great deeds, and now the hour is at hand.

Zebulon
Stay where you are. The time is God's choice, not ours. The king will decide.

Baruch
Listen to the shouts of joy! Let me go with them, father.

Zebulon
You will have many other opportunities. The people always flock to hear loud talkers, and crowd ever to witness showy sights.

Another
Why do you deny him the pleasure? Is not the day come for which we have been longing? Friends have been raised up for Israel.

Zebulon
Never was Mizraim the friend of Israel.

Baruch

Our shame is theirs, and Israel's need is Egypt's.

Zebulon

Naught have we in common with any other folk on earth. Our strength lies in isolation.

The Other

But they will fight for us.

Zebulon

They will fight for themselves. Each nation fights for itself alone.

Baruch

Are we still to be slaves? Shall Zedekiah be a king of slaves, and Zion remain in bondage to Chaldea? Were but Zedekiah a true king!

Zebulon

Silence, I command you. It befits not a boy to lay down the law for kings.

Baruch

It is true that I am young; but who is Jerusalem, if it be not her young men? It was not the cautious elders who built Jerusalem. David, young David, established her towers, and made her great among the nations.

Zebulon

Hold your peace. You have no right to speak in the marketplace.

Baruch

Shall only the cautious elders speak, none but the aged give counsel, that Israel may grow old before her time and God's word decay in our hearts? The moment is ours, and it is for us to take revenge. You have abased yourselves, and we will lift ourselves up; you have faltered, but we will bring fruition; you had peace, and we want war.

Zebulon

What do you know of war? We, the fathers, have known war. In books war is great, but in reality war is a destroyer, a ravisher of life.

Baruch

I fear not war. Let us have done with slavery!

A Voice

Zedekiah hath sworn an oath of peace.

Voices

The oath matters nothing.—Let him break his oath.—No oath need be kept with the heathen.

Other Voices

[Exultant, coming from the street] Abimelech!—Hail Abimelech!—Abimelech, our leader!

[Groups crowd round Abimelech, the general, and acclaim him]

Voices

Abimelech!—Is it true that Egypt offers an alliance? Draw your sword.—Up, march against Ashur.—Gather Israel's forces.—We are ready.—We are ready.

Abimelech

[Speaks to the crowd from the top of the steps] Make ready, people of Jerusalem, for the hour of freedom is at hand.

[The crowd shouts exultantly]

Pharaoh-Necho has offered us the help of his armies. He wishes us to join him in breaking the might of Ashur, and we shall do it, people of Jerusalem.

The Crowd
On against Ashur.—War with Chaldea.—Hail Abimelech!

A Warrior
We shall drive them before us like sheep. They have grown soft in the houses of the women, and their king has never worn harness.

A Voice
That is false.

The Warrior
Who says it is false?

The Voice
I say so. I have been in Babylon and I have seen Nebuchadnezzar. He is a mighty man of valor, and his soldiers have no equals.

Voices
Wretch, you praise our foes.—He is sold to the enemy.—His wife is a Chaldean.—She has gone a-whoring with all the men of Babylon.—Traitor!

The Warrior
[Approaching the speaker] Do you mean to say that we cannot beat them?

The Voice
I say that the Chaldeans are mighty men.

The Warrior
[Pressing closer] Look upon my fist, and say once more that they are better than the men of Israel.

Voices
Say it again.—Tear him to pieces.—Traitor.—Traitor.

The Speaker

[Encircled by a threatening mob, loses courage] I did not say that. All I meant to say was that they are many in number.

Abimelech

Always have our foes been many, and always have we laid them low.

Voices

Who can stand against us?—We have overthrown all our enemies.—None can withstand us.—Death to him who despises our power.

[Messengers hasten from the palace]

The Crowd

[Thronging round them] Whither so fast?—What news do you bear?—Whom do you seek?—What's afoot?

A Messenger

The king has summoned the council.

Voices

War.—He decides for war.—War.

Abimelech

Whom has he summoned?

The Messenger

Imre, the oldest burgher; Nahum, the steward. To you also the summons goes forth.

Abimelech

Waverers and wiseacres are to be my fellow councilors; men who weigh their words overmuch and shrink from deeds. But I have my sword with me, and I will cast it from me if I may not draw it against Ashur. Yours is the hour, people of Jerusalem; I fight in your behalf.

The Crowd
Hail Abimelech.—Hail Abimelech, hail soldier of God.—Hail!

[Abimelech hastens into the palace]

Baruch
Follow him, follow him! The king shall hear our voices. Let us thunder our will beneath the windows of his palace.

Zebulon
I shall disown you if you do not hold your peace. The king has summoned a council, and there must be no clamor to disturb its deliberations.

Baruch
He shall not deliberate. Let him decide! Let him decide for war! We are all for war.

Voices
Yes, all of us.—All of us.—Shout that the king may hear us.

A Voice
Nay, I am not for war, I am not for war.

Voices
Silence.—Traitor.—Another spy.—Who are you?—Down with him.—Who are you?

The Speaker
I am a peasant, and in peace only will my land bear fruit. War comes trampling across my fields. No war for me, I am against it.

Baruch
[Savagely] Shame upon you! May you rot amid your fields and be choked with your fruits! Cursed be he whose courage is measured by his gains, and cursed be he who values his own pitiful life more than the welfare of his country! Israel is our land for tillage. We will manure it with our blood. Are we not happy, brothers, to die for the one God?

The Peasant

Die, then, and let me live. I love the land. This, too, is God's, and he has given it to me for my own.

Baruch

Nothing is given to us for our own. We hold everything in trust from the living God, and must restore everything when the call comes. Now has the call sounded; let us hearken to it gladly. The signs are fulfilled. Where are they who should reveal his words? Where are they who disclose his spirit, who can spur on the slothful and make the deaf hear? Where are the priests, and where the prophets? Why are their voices silent at this hour in Jerusalem?

Voices

Yes.—The prophets.—Where are the priests?

Baruch

To the temple! Nothing must be done without God's word! Let the men of God decide.

Voices

Yes, where are our shepherds? In them is the truth.—Hananiah—Pashur—where are they? Open the temple.—Open the gates.—Hananiah.—Pashur.

[Some of the crowd race up the steps and knock upon the brazen gates. The gates open and Hananiah appears. He is received with fierce acclamations]

Baruch

Hananiah, messenger of God, the people thirst for your speech. Let your words pour forth to kindle our hearts, to make fruitful our wrath, and to direct our aim. The fate of Jerusalem is in your hands.

The Crowd

Pour forth God's word over us.—Reveal the promise.—Say, shall we fight?—Let us know God's will.—Teach the people, messenger of the

Lord, teach the king.—Give utterance to the promise.—Look upon our weakness.—Awaken our courage.

Hananiah

[Standing before the threshold of the temple, speaks with strong emotion] Blessed your questions, blessed your voices, blessed are you, people of Jerusalem, who at length hearken to the cry. For sleep had fallen upon you, Jerusalem; you had been passive in the chains of slavery. The nations have been marching over you as over a drunken man; they have been spitting upon your garments; they have mocked your nakedness. But a call has summoned the sleepers; a message has roused the dreamers; and I will testify to you, now that God has awakened you.

The Crowd

[Breaking into fanatical cries] Listen to him!—We are awakened!—It is true that we have been sleeping.—Tell us, master, is it time?—Say, has the hour struck?

Hananiah

How long will you refrain from deeds, now that God hath awakened you? How long will you remain passive, now that the Lord hath summoned you? God is athirst, for his pitchers are empty; God is anhungered, for his altars are broken; God is cold, for the hangings of the temple have been stolen; God suffers, for the priests of Baal and the servants of Ashtaroth heap scorn upon him! Cast off the yoke, break your chains, raise hosannas, unsheathe your swords. God has awakened you; fight for the Lord!

Baruch

Let hosannas sound! Up, Israel; up Jerusalem, and break the yoke!

The Crowd

Let us break the yoke.—Down with Ashur.—To arms against Nebuchadnezzar.—Unfurl the flag.—Tell us, is it time to start?—War against Ashur.—Say, shall the victory be ours?

Hananiah

The voice of the Lord burns within me. The words come to my mouth like the roaring of the sea, and thus do they sound: "Arise, Israel. I have delivered Ashur into thy hand; clench thy fist, Israel, and break the bones of thy foe! Tread the oppressor beneath thy heels, bring back my stolen goods, deliver me as I deliver thee. Reject those who would counsel thee otherwise; destroy those who would curb thee; pay no heed to the weaklings, and hearken only to the words of my messenger! Hear the words of my messenger, O Israel!"

Jeremiah

[Calling wildly from amid the crowd] Heed him not! Heed him not! Heed him not!

[A tumult ensues, and the crowd draws apart, disclosing Jeremiah in the midst. He tries to make his way up the steps to the place from which Hananiah is speaking]

Voices

Who is that speaking?—What is he saying?—Who is he?

Jeremiah

Do not heed him. Pay no heed to him who speaks through the lips only; reject the lure of his words. Do not listen to the hypocrites who would lead you into slippery places. Do not fall into the snare of the fowlers. Do not listen to the decoy calling to war.

Pashur

[The high priest, wearing full vestments, has appeared on the threshold of the temple] Who speaks in the crowd?

Hananiah

Who speaks against the Lord? Let him show himself in the open.

Jeremiah

[Coming forward] Dismay speaks; concern for Jerusalem cries aloud; the mouth of terror is opened. I speak for Israel, and for the life of Israel.

Voices

Who is he?—I know him not.—He is not one of the prophets.—I know him not.—Who is he?

A Voice

It is Jeremiah, the son of Hilkiah, of the priests in Anathoth.

Voices

Who is Jeremiah?—Who is he?—What do the people of Anathoth want in Jerusalem?—He is the son of Hilkiah.—Who is he?—What does he want?

Pashur

[To Jeremiah, who is mounting the steps] Away from the steps of the temple! The messengers of the Lord, the men of God and the prophets, may alone tread the holy threshold. To none but us is it given to reveal God's will.

Jeremiah

Who dares declare that to him only has the Lord vouchsafed wisdom and the secret of his will? God speaks to men in dreams, and to me likewise has he sent dreams. He has filled my nights with horror, and has awakened me at due time; he has given me a mouth that I may speak and a voice that I may cry aloud. He has breathed dismay into my mind that I may spread it over you like a burning cloth. I will utter my dismay on behalf of Jerusalem; I will cry my cry before the people; I will reveal my dreams.

Baruch

Away with dreamers and interpreters of dreams. The hour needs waking men.

Hananiah

Dreams come to all. Beasts stir in their sleep, and the dreams of slaves are full of visions. Who has anointed you, that you should speak before the temple?

Voices

No.—Let him speak.—We want to hear him.—He is out of his mind.—Let him reveal his dreams.—The marketplace is free to all.—God's house is free. Speak, Jeremiah.

Pashur

Not from the threshold of the temple.

Hananiah

I am the prophet of God, and there is no other prophet in Israel to-day. You shall hear my words, not those of the chatterers in the streets. Scourge the dreamers out of the marketplace.

Baruch

He is a coward, shun his terrors.

Voices

Let him speak.—We want to hear what he has to say.—No, let Hananiah speak.—Perhaps Jeremiah is sent by the Lord.—Why should not we hear him.—Speak, Jeremiah.—What has he dreamed?—Revelation often comes in dreams.—Let him speak, Hananiah.—We can compare their words.— Speak, Jeremiah.

Jeremiah

[From the top of the steps] Brothers in Israel, brothers in Jerusalem, in my dream I heard a storm burst upon the city, and I saw warriors assail our walls. The pillars fell and the battlements were laid low. Fire sat upon the roofs like a red beast devouring our dwellings. No stone was left standing upon another, and the streets were laid waste. I saw the dead lying in heaps upon the ground, so that my heart was turned within me and my mouth was unsealed even in sleep.

Pashur

Madness is crying from the steps of the temple.

Hananiah

The falling sickness afflicts him, and he in turn afflicts us.

Baruch

Down with him.

Voices

No, we want to hear his dreams.—What do they mean?—He is a madman.
—He is a fool.—Away with him!

Jeremiah

But, brothers, when I awakened in the sweat of my body, I mocked
myself even as you mock me now. Did not peace brood over the land;
were not the walls untouched, so that no breeze stirred athwart them? I
went forth from the house full of shame for my own terrors; I sought the
marketplace that I might rejoice in its peace. But when I came thither I
heard shouts of exultation; and my heart broke within me, for the shouts
were clamors for war. Brothers, my soul was bitter as gall, and the words
came to my lips against my will. Tell me, is war so precious that you
should praise it? Is it so kindly that you should long for it? Does it bring
so much good that you should greet it with all the warmth of your heart?
I say unto you, people of Jerusalem, that war is a fierce and evil beast,
one that devours the flesh of the strong and sucks the marrow of the
mighty, crushing towns in its jaws and trampling the land beneath its
hoofs. Those who awaken it, shall not again lay it to sleep; and he who
draws the sword, is like to perish by the sword. Woe, therefore, to the
contentious man who quarrels when there is no need, for he shall come
out upon one way, and flee upon seven. Woe to those who murder peace
with the words of their mouth. Beware of all such, O people of Jerusalem.

Baruch

Beware of cowards, O people of Jerusalem; beware of traitors in the pay
of the enemy.

Hananiah

What promise does he bring? Where is God's word? He speaks for
Babylon and for Baal.

Voices

No, no.—His words are just.—There is much truth in what he says.—Let him deliver his message.—Dreams.—Where is the promise?—Go on.—We want to hear him too.

Jeremiah

Why do you awaken the ravening beast with your shouts. Why do you summon the king of the north to your city? Why do you clamor for war, men of Jerusalem? Did you beget your sons for slaughter, and your daughters for shame? Did you build your houses for destruction by fire, and your walls for the battering ram? Bethink thee, Israel; call a halt ere thou runnest into the darkness, Jerusalem. Is thy slavery so hard, are thy sorrows beyond assuagement? Look around. God's sun shines over the land; the vines bloom in peace; lovers walk happily together; children play unhindered; the moon shines gently over the sleep of Jerusalem. Fire and water keep their appointed places, the storehouses are well filled, and God has his spacious mansion. Say, Israel, is it not well with thee within the walls of Zion; art thou not blithe in the valleys of Sharon; art thou not happy by the blue waters of Jordan? Let it suffice thee to live at peace under God's tranquil gaze. Hold fast to peace, people of Jerusalem.

Zebulon

His words are just! Hail unto him. His speech is golden.

Pashur

Like the gold of Chaldea.

Voices

Yes, he has been bribed.—No, his words are just.—Peace.—We want peace.—He is a traitor.—He is in the pay of Ashur.—Let him speak.—No, Hananiah is right.—Let us listen to Hananiah.

Hananiah

Away with you, away. Go, talk to Samaria, the land of slaves. Deliver your message to Moab, or to the uncircumcised, but not to Israel, God's first-born among the nations.

Baruch

[Menacingly, to Jeremiah] Answer me, in face of the people. Is our slavery to endure? Are we still to pay tribute to Chaldea? Answer me, traitor.

Voices

Yes, yes.—Answer.—Speak.—Are we to go on paying tribute?—Answer.

Jeremiah

Loudly do I speak my mind before the people. It is better to pay tribute of gold to the enemy than tribute of blood to war. It is better to be wise than powerful; it is better to be the servant of God than the ruler of men.

Hananiah

Man of servile obedience, slave of Chaldea, will you deny God's word which commandeth war against the oppressor; will you deny his holy word?

Jeremiah

But it is also written: "In returning and rest shall ye be saved; in quietness and in confidence shall be your strength."

Voices

Yes, thus is it written.—He speaks truth.—His words are the words of wisdom.—Nay, he twists the scripture to his own purpose.

Hananiah

This is written of an unholy war, of dissension among the brethren of Israel. But ours is a holy war, a war of God waged in the everlasting name of Jerusalem, a war of God, a war of God.

Jeremiah

Couple not God's name with war. Not God makes war, but man. No war is holy; no death is holy; life alone is holy.

Baruch

You lie! Life is given us that we may sacrifice it to God. I will offer myself upon his altar, I will fall before his foes, I will die for Israel and for Israel's rule upon earth. Never shall Israel be vanquished so long as all her sons share these thoughts.

Hananiah
Never shall Israel be vanquished while God's stars shine in heaven. If we join forces with Egypt, Babylon will fall into our hands within three months.

Voices
[Exultantly] Within three months.—Hail Hananiah.—Hearken to Hananiah.—Within three months.

Hananiah
Israel will gain the victory over countless thousands.

Baruch
He spreads fear as they spread gold before him.

Voices
Israel shall rule the nations.—Down with Ashur.—War.—War.—Nay, peace.—Peace in Israel.—War.—War.—He is speaking for Ashur.—He is a traitor.—Do those only speak truth who clamor for war?—He has taken bribes.—Let us not decide too quickly.

Baruch
Send the coward to the house of the women!

A Woman
[Spitting on Jeremiah] His company would bring shame on us. That for the man whose cringing is a disgrace! War against Ashur!

Jeremiah
[Flashing out in wrath] Who are you that you crave blood so fiercely? Did you bear children and suckle them only for the tomb? A curse upon the man who thirsts for blood, but seven times accursed be the woman who is eager for war; for war shall devour the fruit of her womb, and the men of Ashur shall cast lots for her and for her raiment. You and such as you

shall be mourners, tearing your cheeks with your nails, and uttering shrill cries of lamentation, you women who spit upon me and revile peace.

Women's Voices
Woe, Woe! Listen to the curse.—Our sons.—Woe, woe!—Man of terror!—Woe!

Baruch
You can frighten women, faint-heart, but not men. Down, down!

Certain Warriors
Down with him. Hunt him into the street.

Hananiah
Close his mouth!

Voices
Away with him!—He frightens women.—Away with him.—He has foretold enough disaster.—My flesh crept while he was speaking.—Let him hold his peace.

Jeremiah
I will not hold my peace, for Jerusalem cries aloud through my mouth. The walls of Jerusalem stand up in my heart, and would fain still stand; the land of Israel blossoms in my soul, and my hope is to safeguard it. Thy own blood calls through me, Jerusalem, that it may not be shed; thy seed, that it may not be scattered; thy stones, that they may not fall; and thy name, that it may not perish. Stand firm, waverer, and gather thy children under thy care; hearken, Jerusalem, to my voice of warning. Hearken, Zion, thou citadel of God. Keep the peace, keep the peace!

Voices
[Fiercely disputing] Yes.—God's peace upon Israel.—Traitor.—He has taken a bribe.—God's peace upon us.—I would fain save my sons.—War.—War against Ashur.—Leave the matter to the king.—He is a traitor.—We want to live at peace.—He is a coward.—He has sold himself to the enemy.

—War.—Peace.—Hananiah speaks the truth.—Nay, Jeremiah speaks the truth.—Break the yoke.—War.—Peace.

[A bustle arises at the entrance to the palace. A number of men come forth. In their midst is Abimelech, swordless]

Voices
[From among the newcomers] Treason.—Treason.—Treason in Israel.

[The dispute around Jeremiah ceases]

Voices
What has happened?—Abimelech.—What has happened?—He comes from the king.—Abimelech.—Look at his angry frown.—Tell us what has happened.

Abimelech
[Standing at the top of the steps beside Jeremiah] Israel has been sold by the weaklings; chaffered away by the hucksters. Imre and Nahum gained the upper hand in the council. They spoke against Egypt, and the king hearkened to their words.

Voices
Down with Nahum.—Treason.—Imre, the dotard.—Traitor.—What was the decision?—What did the king say?—Peace, hail to peace.—God's judgment.

Abimelech
His heart quaileth within him, for he dreads war. He will think the matter over, will take further counsel ere he decide.

Jeremiah
Glory to Zedekiah, girdled with wisdom!

Abimelech

He is hedged about with weakness; old age and fear are his counselors. For my part I threw my sword aside, for no longer will I wear a sword while Zion pays tribute to Ashur.

Baruch

[In ecstasy] Soldier of God, your sword is holy since it flashes for Israel.

Pashur

Blessings upon you that you will have naught to do with hucksters.

Hananiah

Shall we still hesitate? Whose is the hour? Is it that of Nahum, the huckster, and that of Imre, the dotard; or is it your hour, people of Jerusalem? God's hour has come, therefore seize it. To the palace, to the king; let him behold us and hear us. People of Jerusalem, raise your voices, give vent to the breath of your anger. To the palace, to the palace!

Pashur

To the king! Show yourselves to him, people of Jerusalem. To the king and to victory! Such is God's will.

Voices

To the king!—To the palace!—To victory!

Jeremiah

[Springing forward to block the entry to the porch of pillars] Keep the peace, keep the peace; you are murdering Jerusalem.

Baruch

[Drawing his sword] Here's for him who still speaks of peace.

Hananiah

Cut him down!

Pashur

Down with the traitor!

Jeremiah

Help me, friends of God; help me to save Jerusalem.

Baruch

For the last time! Let us pass in to the king. [He endeavors to push Jeremiah aside]

Jeremiah

[Resists and shouts at the top of his voice] No step will I yield to folly! Peace! God's peace be upon Israel.

[Baruch cuts him down, and Jeremiah falls bleeding to the foot of the steps]

The Crowd

[Scattering in horror] Murder.—They have killed him.—Murder.—Who is it?—Jeremiah.—They have killed him.—Woe.—Why use force?—Why kill the prophets?—Justice has been dealt on the liar.—To the king, to the king!

[Baruch stands thunderstruck with lowered sword]

Hananiah

[Shouts exultantly] May such be the fate of all faint-hearts, all slaves of Chaldea, all hirelings of Ashur! To the palace, to the king. Save Israel, deliver Jerusalem.

Abimelech

Death to traitors! Vengeance on Ashur!

Pashur

God has struck him down.

Hananiah

God's thunderbolt has fallen on the liar.

The Crowd

[After its brief pause of consternation, begins to flow into the porch of pillars of the palace] To the king.—Let Israel rule the nations.—War.—War against Ashur.—Down with the traitors.—To the king.—God is on our side.—Down with Ashur.—Freedom.—Freedom. [Rejoicing they stream into the palace]

[Jeremiah still lies in a swoon at the base of the steps, none heeding him. The crowd passes over him in a flood, leaving him like jetsam among the stones. Baruch, who, in his bewilderment, was swept along by the mob, has struggled back from among them. Slowly, as if driven by an inner force, he comes down to the swooning man, bends over him, feels his brow, and listens for his breath]

Baruch

Jeremiah, speak, Jeremiah, if you are still alive. [He raises Jeremiah into a sitting posture]

Jeremiah

[His eyes still closed, not yet himself, speaks hesitatingly] The fiery cloud has fallen. Fire is raging through the town. Woe is me!

Baruch

Keep still a moment, that I may wipe the blood from your eyes.

Jeremiah

Away! Your face was full of hatred towards me. Your eyes flashed fiercely. Was it not you who struck me down?

Baruch

I indeed it was who drew sword upon you in anger, but the blade turned in my hand so that I struck you with the flat only. I rejoice thereat, for I drew upon an unarmed man. I will pay blood-money. Let me staunch your wound.

42

Jeremiah

Let the blood flow. Would that mine alone were to flow in Jerusalem. [Half rising] What has become of the crowd? The marketplace is empty. Have they gone to the palace, gone to force war upon the king? Where are they?

Baruch

Compose yourself ...

Jeremiah

They have gone. It is too late. Curse upon you for that you felled me to the ground. More, far more, than me have you slain. Not my blood alone has been shed, but the blood of all Israel. Through you, Zion has been broken and destroyed. You have killed the watchman, and they are raging in the holy places of the Lord. Let me rise. Avaunt, murderer of Israel!

Baruch

What do you wish to do?

Jeremiah

[In febrile excitement] Help me, help me to my feet. You struck me down, so now you must help me. Perhaps there is still time. [Distant shouts are heard from the palace] Their jubilation means death; their joy means destruction. Too late! Too late! For Jerusalem's sake I must give warning. Your aid! I must go to him. The hour calls. [He struggles to his feet]

Baruch

[Confused] Whither away? You are still too weak to do anything.

Jeremiah

Let me testify against Hananiah, against Pashur; against those who would lure to war; against the people. I must cry the words of peace ...

Baruch

Will you make the attempt once again, alone against them all? Great, indeed, is the force that drives you. Steadfastly did you face my sword, you whom I had despised as a coward, whom I had proclaimed a faint-heart before the people. But in the strength of your will you are ready to defy death, proving yourself a mighty man of valor.

Jeremiah

If you reverence me, then help me. Help me to cry aloud. Help me to save Zion from destruction.

Baruch

[Supporting him] I will help you, Jeremiah, against my will, for you have in you a power which compels me. I had believed you a weakling, and therefore did I oppose you as one who shunned action and favored the easy path of peace.

Jeremiah

The easy path of peace! Do you fancy that peace is not action, that peace is not the action of all actions? Day by day you must wrest it from the mouths of liars and from the hearts of men. You must stand alone against the multitude; for clamor is always on the side of the many, and the liar has ever the first word. The meek must be strong; those who desire peace are continually at war.

Baruch

But you will not go alone?

Jeremiah

I must go, I must go. I must make my words good. Empty is the speech of him who will not stand by it with his life. Let me publish my visions; let me proclaim my warning before the king.

Baruch

I would fain go with you, would fain do what you are doing, for it is borne in on me that you are beginning a great work.

Jeremiah

You would walk with me? But did you not resist me with your will and with your sword?

Baruch

You are too strong for me, and I who stood up against you wish to help you now. Your blood has won me to your cause. I will do what you do, for I have faith in you, Jeremiah, who faced my sword so steadfastly.

Jeremiah

You believe in me, against the priests and the prophets who deny me, against the people and the city?

Baruch

I believe in you, for you have shed your blood for your words.

Jeremiah

You believe in me when I myself hardly believe in my own dreams. Is it true, boy?

Baruch

I believe in you, for I saw you stand steadfast against death. Your will is my will.

Jeremiah

[Greatly moved] You believe in me, you who wounded me, who resisted me to the uttermost? You are the first to believe in me, you whose very name is unknown to me.

Baruch

I am Baruch, the son of Zebulon of Gilead.

Jeremiah

No longer will you be any man's son, if you believe in me. Despised and rejected will you be, should you follow me. He who would shine in the word, must burn in the flames. Think well, Baruch. You are little more than a boy. You have shed my blood, shall I therefore shed yours?

Baruch

Let me go with you, for the sake of Jerusalem.

Jeremiah

For the sake of Jerusalem! Indeed and indeed Jerusalem needs help in this hour. Come, then, Baruch, first-born of my faith, son of my anguish, support me that we may testify together. My anguish shall be turned against the king, my sorrow shall be thundered in his ears. Aid me, aid me against king and people.

Baruch

I will go with you.

[Exultant shouts nearer at hand]

Jeremiah

Woe, woe! When the mob rejoices, disaster is afoot.

Baruch

They are streaming forth from the palace.

Jeremiah

Forward, let us meet them. Lend me the strength of your arm, for I am still weak.

Baruch

The king is among them. He carries a naked sword. They are making for the temple.

Jeremiah

Help me forward. There is still time.

Baruch

The clamor echoes through the marketplace. Hananiah is dancing before them even as David danced before the ark. The war-makers have triumphed. It is too late. Give way before them. Hide yourself. It is too late.

Jeremiah

It is never too late. Let me forth to encounter them.

Baruch

What would you do? Let me go instead, for I am young and strong.

Jeremiah

I would brandish the word against them like a sword. I would turn the king's heart. Let me go to him.

[Shouting and singing, the crowd streams out of the palace, down the steps, and then up again towards the temple. All are in a frenzy, shouting for war and for victory]

Hananiah

[Drunken with excitement, leading the way to the temple] Open the gates. Throw the gates wide. The king will swear before the altar the oath of alliance against Ashur!

Voices

Hail to the alliance!—Day of promise!—Slavery is overthrown!—Down with Ashur!—Hail Zedekiah!—Victory, victory!—Israel shall rule the nations.—God is on our side.

[King Zedekiah, followed by the Egyptian envoys, has come out of the palace. He bears a drawn sword. His expression is grave. Amid the exultant crowd he seems oppressed with thought. Scarcely heeding the tumult and the acclamations, he makes for the temple with slow strides. Suddenly, above the clamor of the multitude, rises the voice of Jeremiah]

Jeremiah

Zedekiah, Zedekiah, sheathe thy sword.

[Disorder in the crowd; the cries are stilled. The king, standing on the steps of the temple, looks round for the speaker]

Jeremiah

[Shouting yet more loudly] Sheathe thy sword, Zedekiah! Thus wilt thou save Jerusalem. Give peace to Israel, God's peace.

The Crowd

[Vociferating wildly] War! War upon Ashur!—Who is the speaker?—He is sold to the enemy.—Down with all traitors.—Israel shall rule the nations. —War, war!

[The voice of Jeremiah is drowned amid the general uproar. He is thrust aside, and Baruch has difficulty in protecting him. With redoubled energy the crowd continues to shout in an ecstasy around the king. Zedekiah stands awhile, still trying to find the one who had called on him to sheathe the sword. For a moment, indeed, he lowers his weapon, and seems to be looking round for help. But, amid fanatical cries of the populace, the gates are opened. After a moment's further hesitation, Zedekiah raises his sword once more, and with earnest mien mounts the last steps and disappears into the temple]

RUMORS

SCENE THREE

Because ye speak this word, behold, I will make my words in thy mouth fire, and this people, wood, and it shall devour them. Jeremiah V, 14.

SCENE THREE

The same square in front of the temple and the king's palace. Groups of idlers, men and women, loiter upon the steps, some sitting and some standing. In the streets and in the porch of pillars there is the usual coming and going of persons working and conversing.

A Man

[One of the larger group on the steps] I have it for certain that there has been a great battle between Nebuchadnezzar and Pharaoh.

Another Man

I have heard the same report. A messenger has come.

A Voice

That means nothing. Messengers are always coming to the palace.

The Second Man

But I have spoken to him. I'm sure of it.

The Voice

Have you spoken to the messenger?

The Second Man

No, it was Aphitor, the king's scribe. He told me that a battle had begun, a great battle.

The First Man

A mighty battle, such as there has never been before within the memory of man, Egypt against Nebuchadnezzar.

Voices

May the heavens crush him, the accursèd.—Egypt is all-powerful.—Our army is there too.—They will know how to deal with him, the man of pride.

A Voice

God will break him, for God is on our side.

Another Voice

The Egyptians are strong, and Nebuchadnezzar will not be able to withstand them.

A Third Voice

Nebuchadnezzar is likewise strong. They say ...

A Fourth Voice

[Interrupting] Let them say, the faint-hearts. Who cares what they say?

Third Voice

They say that his warriors are like a swarm of locusts.

Another Voice

Warriors! His men are no warriors! Small in stature are they like boys, and unhandy with their swords. My sister's husband has seen many of them. Among the women they are men, but they are not men in battle. [Laughter]

Voices

Pharaoh will destroy them.—He will sweep them like chaff from the threshing-floor.—Long live Pharaoh!

Others

[Hearing the shouts and coming to join the group] What is he saying about Pharaoh?

A Voice

Pharaoh is fighting a great battle against Nebuchadnezzar.

Other Voices

He will conquer.—He will set us free.—Long live Pharaoh.—Pharaoh for ever.—They shall grave him a tablet of fine gold.—Long live Pharaoh, the conqueror of Ashur.

Newcomers
[Eager to know what is afoot] What is it? What has happened?

One of the Recent Comers
Pharaoh has defeated Nebuchadnezzar.

Voices
Hail Pharaoh-Necho!—Is it true? I must go home and tell my wife.—Hail Pharaoh-Necho!

A Voice
But we have no certain news yet.

Other Voices
What do you mean by saying the news is not certain?—Can you doubt it?—I have always known that God would strengthen our arms.—Victory is ever on God's side.—None can stand against us.

One of the Group
[Hastening away, shouting as he goes] The victory is ours. Pharaoh has defeated Nebuchadnezzar.

[Hearing these words, idlers in the square flock to join the group on the steps]

Voices
They are talking of a victory.—Is it true that Pharaoh has vanquished Nebuchadnezzar?—Quite true.—No one really knows yet.—It is absolutely certain.—Who says so?—Everyone says so.—The king's scribe says so.

A Man
[Detaching himself from the crowd, runs away shouting] Victory! Victory at last. Hail Pharaoh. I must get home with the news. Victory over Ashur.

The Crowd

[Swelling in numbers, growing more enthusiastic as it is enheartened by its own clamor] It was God's will that we should begin this war.—Hail Zedekiah!—Now we must conquer all the others.—Israel shall rule the nations.—A sacrifice on the altar.—Give praise unto God, for that he has cast down our enemies.—They shall be our bondsmen.—My heart has thirsted for this hour.

A Voice

A messenger is coming from the gate of the city.

The Crowd

[Making a rush in the direction of the last voice] A messenger.—A messenger.—Who said so?—He comes from beyond the walls.—What news does he bring? Where is he?

[A messenger, drenched with sweat and gasping for breath, struggles through the crowd]

Voices

Tell us the news.—Pharaoh is victorious.—What has happened to Nebuchadnezzar?—How many have been slain?

The Messenger

Let me be. Make room. My message is for the king.

Voices

Don't be so churlish.—Let us hear one word at least.—Has he fled?—Tell us the news.—Let the man alone.—His business is with the king.—Just a word.

The Messenger

[Breaking loose] Let me be, let me be. You will learn soon enough. My message is urgent, and for the king. [Exit messenger.]

Voices

What did he say? The message was urgent.—What did he say?

A Voice

He said we should soon hear, but that he must go to the king at once.

Another Voice

That is good news.

A Third Voice

Wherefore good?

The Second Voice

Would the bearer of evil tidings be in so desperate a hurry?

Voices

True, true.—The king will pay him a silver shekel for every word.—He is eager to earn the messenger's guerdon.—He brings tidings of victory.— Victory!—Good news.—Victory!

Some Newcomers

What has happened? Why are you shouting?

Voices

Victory!—Victory!—A messenger has come.—He brings tidings of victory. —Nebuchadnezzar is beaten.—A great and glorious victory.—God be praised.—Alleluia! The news is certain.—Victory.—Victory!

A Voice

It must be a mighty victory.

A Second Voice

Were it otherwise he would not have been so secret.

A Third Voice

They grudge us the news.

A Newcomer

[Pressing forward] Is it true? Is Nebuchadnezzar slain? So the word runs from street to street.

Voices

Yes, slain is the oppressor.—Nay, the news is not yet confirmed.—But the messenger said so; he told us that Nebuchadnezzar had been killed in his tent.—Myriads of the enemy have fallen with him, God be thanked.—The oppressor is slain.—Alleluia!

An Old Man

But all that the messenger said was ...

Voices

He told us of the victory.—Why are you still in doubt?—I wish we could exterminate these faint-hearts.—I heard it myself.—So did I.—So did I.—The messenger said that Nebuchadnezzar had been killed in his tent.—No, he never said that.—Yes.—No.—But undoubtedly he brought tidings of victory.—Israel is free.—Free!

The Old Man

I tell you I was standing quite close to him. I could hear every word he said.

Voices

Your ears and your heart are deafened.—These kill-joys should themselves be killed.—Let us don our festal attire.—Out of the way, chatterbox.

A Voice

Hananiah was a true prophet. Wise were we to heed his words, and not to hearken to those who declared that the temple would fall ...

Another Voice

Who said that Ashur would lay Zion low ...

A Third Voice
Who said that our maids would be ravished by the Chaldeans ...

First Voice
To the temple, to the temple. Let us give thanks there to God, and to
Hananiah, his prophet!

Voices
No, let us wait here, for the king will come soon.—Who said so?—Kings
always appear in public after a victory.—The king will go to the temple.—
The king must be the first to offer a sacrifice.—All right, let us stay
here.—Let us send for drums and cymbals to celebrate the victory.—We
will dance like David before the ark.—God is once more showing his love
for Jerusalem.—Fetch the dancers.—Summon the women.—Call the
trumpeters and the lute-players.—Let us make merry and give praise to
the king of kings.

[The crowd sways to and fro joyfully, in movements like those of a
troubled sea. Groups form, dissolve, and reform. The general mood is one
of expectation and impatience. Jeremiah and Baruch enter from a side
street, and endeavor to make their way through the press]

One of the Crowd
[Laughing] Look! There he comes! Jeremiah.

Others
[Giving vent to their high spirits] Hail to the revealer!—Lo, the prophet
draws nigh.—Let us welcome the destroyer of Jerusalem.—Behold the
mob orator.—Come and join us.

[Some of the crowd form a circle round Jeremiah and Baruch, bowing
before them in mock veneration.]

One of the Crowd
[With a profound reverence] Hail anointed of the Lord!

The Others

Hail Elijah!—Hail revealer.—Hail mighty man of valor! Hail Jeremiah, the prophet!

Jeremiah

[Standing his ground, gloomily] What would ye of me?

Baruch

Hold no converse with them. Mockery is on their lips, and derision in their glance.

One of the Crowd

Deign to bestow upon us wisdom and revelation.

Another

We would fain ask you whether our daughters shall keep their virginity.

A Third

Prithee be patient, and allow the walls of Jerusalem to remain standing yet awhile.

Jeremiah

[With conviction] What would ye of me? This is no time for jesting, when blood flows and war hangs over Israel.

The First Speaker

The war is finished, and we can make merry once more.

The Second Speaker

What has become of your king from the north? Tell us, revealer, where does he tarry?

Jeremiah

What has confused your senses? Are you all mad? Can the war already be over when it is hardly begun?

Baruch

Hold no speech with them. He makes himself a mock who speaks with mockers.

First Speaker

Jeremiah knows nothing about it yet! The prophet knows nothing.

Second Speaker

He does not know what happened yesterday, and yet he would tell us what will happen to-morrow.

Jeremiah

What is it that I do not yet know? What makes you so joyful? It must be something of ill omen.

First Speaker

He says it is something of ill omen. It is that, in very truth, for your wishes.

Second Speaker

Your king is slain and welters in his blood.

Jeremiah

Nebuchadnezzar is slain? Ashur is vanquished?

First Speaker

Even so, all-knower. Hananiah's word has been fulfilled.

Second Speaker

Rend your raiment and clip your beard. Israel is victorious.

Third Speaker

Bury yourself, prophet. Cut out your tongue. Nebuchadnezzar is dead, but Zion endureth for ever.

Jeremiah

[Greatly moved] Nebuchadnezzar dead? Is it true, it is certain? Tell me, and do not jest in matters of such moment.

First Speaker

He still doubts! Weep, prophet, weep!

Second Speaker

I will cry it aloud in your ears; dead is Nebuchadnezzar; overthrown are his chariots; scattered are his armies. Israel is saved.

Jeremiah

[Remains motionless for a moment. Then he spreads his arms wide, drawing a deep breath of joyful relief. Dropping his arms, he speaks fast and almost exultantly] Blessed be God. I thank thee, all-good, that thou hast brought my dreams to shame, that thou hast saved Jerusalem. Better, assuredly that I should be fooled by my illusions than that the city should be laid waste by the foe. Blessings upon God's name.

First Speaker

Yea, all-knower, God is more merciful than you; he loves us and gladdens our hearts.

Second Speaker

What will your next revelation be? Into which corner will you creep, mole? Whom will you now lead astray?

Third Speaker

Whom will you now deceive, deceiver?

A Fourth Speaker

[With feigned anger, to the others] How irreverently you speak to the messenger of the Lord! Let us kiss the hem of his garment; let us pay honor to his visions!

Voices

[Mingled with laughter] Prophesy to us Elijah.—Instruct us further, all-knower.—Happy the man who puts his trust in Jeremiah.—Where did you pick up that fledgling that chirps at your heels?—Prophesy, Jeremiah; prophesy disaster; mountains of disaster.

Jeremiah

[Suddenly breaking forth into speech] A miracle has happened, people of Jerusalem, a miracle which delivers you from death, and instead of trembling with fear, you make merry. Hardly an hour ago, you were racked with anxiety; your hearts are still quaking, and yet you are already beginning to give tongue. Woe unto you, that your first cry, when the cord is loosed from your necks, should be one of folly and presumption.

Baruch

Speak not with them. Folly alone holds converse with fools.

Second Speaker

Stop your ears as you may, I will cry aloud in my joy: "The victory is ours, the victory is ours!"

Jeremiah

[Addressing one of them] Where have you conquered? Whom have you defeated, that you should strut in the marketplace? There is no blood on your sword. [To another] Show the scar of the wound you received at the battle front! You have all been about your business in the city, have all lain in safety beside your wives at night. What have you and such as you to do with the victory of the Egyptians, with the deeds of foreign fighters? Bow your knees humbly, for the victory is not your work.

Voices

Egypt's victory is Israel's victory.—We are Israel.—His very rage shows that the victory is ours.

Jeremiah

But it is not yours, nor yours, nor yours, you who now swell with pride, battening on the deeds of others. The soldiers have won the victory, not you! Meekly went they forth, to deal death and to suffer it; their backs were bent beneath the weight of their weapons; the shadow of death fell across their path, and all but the strongest fainted by the way. Where they ploughed with naked limbs, you would fain harvest pride. Abandoned wretches, you crave to quench your thirst with their blood. Alas that they have conquered for you and your hateful arrogance!

Voices

Alas that they have conquered, did you hear him? Let us rend our garments, for that we have conquered. Let us strew ashes on our heads, for that Nebuchadnezzar is slain.

Jeremiah

[His wrath blazing up] Verily, O people, to be among you is to dwell among scorpions; but I say unto you that your laughter shall wither more quickly than the blossoms of the vine. God has been gracious to you. Again has he saved Jerusalem; yet not for your laughter, but for the sake of those who are humble in spirit. You will not acknowledge him in his gentleness, men of evil. So be it; ere long shall you acknowledge him in his wrath. Like a curtain shall he rend your laughter asunder, and in your terror your eyes shall become fixed like stones. Your joy then must you put behind you, Jerusalem, for the hour of retribution is at hand, and terrible is the doom that awaits you.

Voices

The walls shall crumble.—The virgins shall weep.—We have heard it all before.—Zion shall perish.—Jeremiah, Jeremiah, you alone are wise among fools.—To him our rejoicing is bitter as gall.—Do you hear the cracking of the walls?

Jeremiah

Do you scorn the messenger of doom? But the avenger is at hand, who shall purge you of your accursèd pride; drawn is the sword which shall hew away your presumption; the bearer of evil tidings is afoot; he is running, he is running; his swift footsteps lead towards Jerusalem. Already he is at hand, the messenger of fear, the messenger of terror; his words will fall on you like the blows of a hammer; even now he is entering the gate.

Voices

Go home, Jeremiah.—Sate yourself with your own venom, and do not vomit it forth upon our joy.

A Voice

[In the background] A messenger! He is coming from Moria gate.

The Crowd

[Again rushing in the direction of the voice] A messenger? Where is he? He brings further news of the victory.

Jeremiah

[Trembling with fear] The messenger! The messenger!

A Voice

He runs hitherward from the gate, and he reels like a drunken man from weariness.

Voices

Where is he?—Here he comes. [Messenger enters. The crowd surrounds him as he tries to hasten to the palace and sinks to the ground exhausted] Hail you who bring tidings of victory.—Hail.—Tell us your news.

The Messenger

[So breathless he can hardly speak, tries to rise and make his way forward] Room, room, let me go to the king.

Voices

Just a word.—How did Nebuchadnezzar die?

The Messenger

Are you all struck with madness? Why this jubilation in Jerusalem? To arms! To arms! Let me pass to the king.

Voices

What has happened?—Is Nebuchadnezzar still alive?—Pharaoh has beaten him.—Why this call to arms?

The Messenger

He draws near with all his forces. Nebuchadnezzar is close at hand. Hardly could I outrun his riders. To arms, to arms! Sentinels to the walls.

Voices

What does the man say?—Who has been beaten?—Where is Pharaoh?— You don't know what you are talking about.—Get him some water.— Nebuchadnezzar alive?—It is impossible.—What has become of the Egyptians?

The Messenger

Water! I am worn out. The Egyptians have been routed. Necho has made peace, and must pay tribute to Ashur. Nebuchadnezzar is coming; his riders are at my heels. I must to the king.

[Some of the crowd help the Messenger to the palace]

Voices

[From the back] What did he say?—Are the Chaldeans beaten?—Why does not the man tell us what has happened?

[Anxiety gradually spreads through the crowd, and the tumult of rejoicing is stilled. In their stupefaction all are mute for a while, and then terrified voices break the silence]

The Crowd

Impossible!—It cannot be true.—The man is a liar.—He was drunk.—Nay, he was only staggering from fatigue.—He said the horsemen were hard at his heels.—The whole story is false.—The messenger had not the mien of a liar.—It cannot be true.—God would never allow such a thing to happen.

A Voice

[Loudly] Pharaoh has betrayed us.

Other Voices

[Quickly and angrily taking up the cry] Pharaoh has betrayed us.—A curse upon Pharaoh.—Egypt has sworn a peace.—A curse upon Mizraim.—The Egyptians are traitors.

A Voice

I have always said that we should never form an alliance with Egypt.

Voices

So did I.—So did I.—We all said so.—Accursèd be Pharaoh.—What will happen to us now?—Alas for Israel.—My wife.—My children.—I warned you what would happen.—So did I.

A Man

[Rushing in] To arms! To arms! Close the gates, Nebuchadnezzar and his hordes are at hand. The advance guard has already reached Hebron.

Voices

Hebron did he say?—To arms!—Nay, peace, peace! Let us march out against him.—All is lost.—From the very first I told you what would happen.

One of the Crowd

[Pointing to Jeremiah who leans brokenly against a pillar, his face hidden] Look, there is the man.

Voices

What?—Who?—What do you mean?

The Same Man

It is his doing. He summoned them. He announced the coming of the messenger. His curse has fallen upon us.

Voices

Who?—Jeremiah!—Who is it?—It is Jeremiah, he has cursed us.—It is indeed his doing.—He prayed for Nebuchadnezzar's victory.—He is sold to the enemy.—Tear him to pieces.—Touch him not; he foretold what would happen; he is a true prophet.—He has been bribed.—See how he stands there brooding.

The Same Man
He hides his face lest we should see his laughter. But he makes merry too soon. Zion still stands; Jerusalem shall endure for ever.

[A herald comes hastily from the palace]

Voices
A herald.—A messenger from the king.—Silence.

[The crowd gathers round the steps to hear the herald's announcement]

The Herald
A message from the king! The enemy is about to attack Jerusalem. The Chaldeans are at the gates. Let every man able to bear arms make ready to fight; women must fashion arrows. All that are sick and weakly must leave the city. Let every man store what food he may in his house lest hunger overcome us. For our walls can withstand attack; Baal can do naught against Jehovah, nor can Ashur prevail against Zion.

The Crowd
True, true.—We will make ready.—God is on our side.—To arms!

The Herald
Let none hold back; let none be faint-hearted. Who speaks of fear, him shall ye put to the sword; who talks of flight, him shall ye chase beyond the walls. Ye may not gather in the streets; each shall keep his own house, ready for the fight. Up, Israel! Gather your forces, fearing nothing, for Jerusalem endureth for ever!

The Crowd
[Again in tumult] Jerusalem endureth for ever.—To arms.—I must fetch my sword.—Up, against Ashur.—Let us take heart.—To the walls.—We shall break them.—Jerusalem endureth for ever.

[The crowd disperses in confusion, so that the square is rapidly emptied, and the noise is followed by silence. Jeremiah slowly draws himself up, and, still hiding his face, ascends the steps of the temple. Baruch follows him]

Baruch

Whither away, master? Do not leave your faithful disciple.

Jeremiah

I must go alone to seek light from the Lord. He made me deliver a sign before the people. Nevertheless, Baruch, I cannot believe that the faces in my ghastly visions are truly from God. Would that I could feel assured they are all illusion, and not the message of God's spirit. Woe indeed if I be chosen as revealer and if my dreams be true.

Baruch

You are chosen, master. It has been made plain to me in this hour. The sign came to you from God. The spirit and the power of the prophets are upon you.

Jeremiah

[Still mounting the steps, flees before him, repelling Baruch with his hands] Say not that I am chosen. Tempt me not! For Israel's sake, for Jerusalem's sake, it is impossible that my words can be true. Far better for me to bear the laughter and the scorn of the people, than that this message of terror should be fulfilled. Rather let me be proved liar and fool, than the prophet of such a truth. May I be thy victim Lord, and not this city. Let me disappear into the darkness of oblivion, if thy towers may still shine, O Jerusalem. May my words vanish like smoke, so long as thou endurest, eternal city. God forget me, if he will but remember thee. I will kneel before his altar praying him to give me the lie; I will beseech him to prove my message false. Pray with me, Baruch, that I be known for a liar in Jerusalem.

[Jeremiah, humbly bending his head, goes up the last steps into the porch of pillars of the temple. Without moving, Baruch gazes after him until he disappears]

THE WATCH ON THE RAMPARTS

SCENE FOUR

Again the word of the Lord came unto me, saying: ... When I bring the sword upon a land, if the people of the land take a man from among them, and set him for their watchman, ... if the watchman see the sword come, and blow not the trumpet, and the people be not warned, and the sword come, and take any person from among them, ... his blood will I require at the watchman's hand. Ezekiel XXXIII, 1-6.

SCENE FOUR

On the ramparts of Jerusalem. The walls, of hewn stone, surround the town. In the background is the starry sky, and faint in the distance the valley with hazy outlines and lights twinkling here and there. The masonry shines in the moonlight. On the wall two sentries march up and down. Their faces are shadowed by their helmets; their spears gleam as they move. Though the hour is late and midnight approaches, a few civilians have ventured on to the wall and are looking out into the distance.

A Woman
It is bedtime. You will see the wretches soon enough in the morning. Do come home; this may be our last quiet night.

A Man
How can one sleep when the enemy is arrayed against us? My heart has been heavier than lead since I have been standing here; and yet I cannot leave. It seems as if I were forced to remain in the flood which is rising to overwhelm us. Last night and to-day the horsemen have been streaming across the plain. Again and again we thought that all must have come, but still there came more and yet more, as if whole countries had been emptied like sacks of grain; while the spears were as the stalks of the corn in number.

Another
Already have they pitched their tents, so that a white forest now stands in the valley.

A Third
Alas, they are settling down for the siege.

A Fourth
They must have come with the speed of the wind. Yesterday they were still at Bethel, and to-day they have already encircled Zion.

The First Man
Terrible is the might of Ashur. God help us all.

The Woman
Look at the glow in the north, like a pillar rising heavenward.

Second Man
That is where Samaria lies.

Third Man
'Tis a pillar of fire that rises heavenward. Samaria has fallen.

Voices
Alas!—It is not possible.—Samaria is a strong fortress, within a triple wall.—Nay, it is certainly Samaria.

A Voice
Look there to the east, another pillar of fire. That must be Gilgal.

Another Voice
They are ravaging the countryside like a hurricane. Fierce is the wrath of Ashur.

Another Voice
Never should we have entered into a struggle with such as they.

Voices
Who began it?—Not we.—Not I.—It was the king.—It was the priests.—We wanted to live at peace with them.

A Voice
Egypt lured us on, and then betrayed us.

Voices
Yes, it was Egypt.—It was Pharaoh.—A curse upon Pharaoh.—The Egyptians have sold us to the enemy, have abandoned us to our misery.—

Where are the fifty thousand bowmen they promised? We are alone.—All is lost.

Another Voice

Woe, Jerusalem, Jerusalem. Thou art given over to thine enemies, and those who hate thee are showing their teeth.

First Sentry

[Fiercely interrupting] Away with you! Why are you loitering on the walls? Home to your wives, and to bed. We stand guard for you.

A Man

We want to see …

First Sentry

There is nothing to see. You have been clamoring for Ashur, and now Ashur has come. Leave it to us men-at-arms to chase them home again. For yourselves, go sleep, or pray if you cannot sleep.

A Man

But tell us …

First Sentry

Naught to tell. There has been too much talking already; the time has come for blows. Away, away!

[The two sentries roughly clear the loiterers from the wall. The crowd disappears in the darkness down the steps leading from the wall into the shadow. When all have gone, quiet reigns. In the white moonlight the sentries stand like figures of brass]

First Sentry

They give way to despair at the first gleam of an enemy's spear. They must not be allowed to talk like that.

Second Sentry

One who is afraid and cannot master his fear must perforce speak. It is of no use, and yet it gives relief.

First Sentry

Let them sleep, not chatter.

Second Sentry

Sleep is not man's servant. Vainly do we summon sleep to a couch of sorrow. To-night many hold vigil and look forth into the moonlight.

First Sentry

In any case, those alone should speak who wear a sword. We stand guard for all.

[The two sentries are silent for a while, marching to and fro]

Second Sentry

[Stands and listens] Do you hear?

First Sentry

What?

Second Sentry

The sound is very faint, but the breeze bears it to us. When I was in Joppa, for the first time I heard in the night the distant murmur of the waves. Such a sound rises now from the plain. They are there in their thousands, moving quietly, but the air is stirred by the rolling wheels and the clashing arms. A whole nation must be afoot, falling upon Israel. The noise echoes from our walls like the noise of the sea.

First Sentry

[Obdurately] I refuse to hear anything but my orders. I care not what wheels roll, or noises stir.

Second Sentry

Why does God hurl the nations against one another? There is room for all beneath the skies. There is still plenty of land unploughed; many forests still await the axe. Yet men turn their ploughshares into swords, and hew living flesh with their axes. I cannot understand, I cannot understand.

First Sentry

It has always been so.

Second Sentry

But must it always be so? Why does God wish the nations to fight?

First Sentry

The nations want war for its own sake.

Second Sentry

What are nations? Are not you one of our nation, am not I another? Are not our wives, your wife and mine, part of this same people? Did any of us want war? I stand here armed with a spear, not knowing against whom it is to be turned. Down there in the darkness, unwitting, waits the man for whom it is destined. I know him not, have never seen his face, or the breast I must pierce with death. In the enemy's camp another perchance warms his hands at the camp fire, the man who is to kill the father of my children. He has never seen me, and I have never done him harm. We are strangers, like trees in the forest. They grow quietly and bear their blossoms. But we rage furiously one against the other with axe and with spear, until our blood runs like resin, and therewith the life oozes forth. What puts death between the nations? What is it which sows hatred when there is room and to spare for life, and when there is abundant scope for love? I cannot understand, I cannot understand!

First Sentry

These things must be God's will, for they have always happened. I question no further.

Second Sentry

This crime cannot be God's will. He has given us our lives that we may live them. Everything that men do not understand they describe as God's will. War does not come from God. Whence comes it then?

First Sentry

How can I tell whence it comes? I know that there is war, and that it is useless to chatter about it. I do my duty; sharpen my spear, not my tongue.

[For a time they are silent once more, gazing out into the white stillness. From a great distance come the words of the challenge "Samson guard us," scarcely audible at first. Then the sound grows louder, still coming from unseen sentries. At length the words "Samson guard us," loud and clear from the next post. Our two sentries take up the challenge, and it is heard with diminishing loudness as it passes on round the wall. Again all is still. The two sentries stand silent in the moonlight, their faces shadowed by their helmets]

Second Sentry

Know you aught of the Chaldeans?

First Sentry

I know that they are our enemies, that they are attacking our homes.

Second Sentry

I am not thinking about that. Have you ever seen any of them close at hand; do you know their customs and their country?

First Sentry

I have been told that they are cruel as wild cats and venomous as serpents. It is said that they sacrifice their children to idols of copper and lead. But I have never set eyes on a Chaldean.

Second Sentry

Nor I. Too many mountains tower skyward between Jerusalem and Babylon; there are rivers to cross, and more country than a man can march over in many weeks. The very stars in the sky are different, and yet the men of Ashur are arrayed against us and we against them. What do they covet from us? If I were to question one of them, all he could tell me would doubtless be that in his house as in mine are wife and children lying upon straw. I believe if I could talk things over with such a man we should understand one another well enough. Often I feel that I should like to summon one of them, to hold out a friendly hand, so that we could have a heart to heart talk.

First Sentry

You must not do that.

Second Sentry

Wherefore not?

First Sentry

They are our enemies and it is our duty to hate them.

Second Sentry

Why should I hate them if my heart knows no reason for hatred?

First Sentry

They began the war; they were the aggressors.

Second Sentry

Yes, that is what we say in Jerusalem. In Babylon, perchance, they tell another story. If we could talk things over with them, we might get some light on the question.

First Sentry

You must not talk with them. Our duty is to strike them down. Such are our orders, and we must obey.

Second Sentry

My reason tells me that I must not converse with them, but in my soul I feel that I must. Whom do we serve by compassing their death?

First Sentry

What a question, simpleton! We serve God, and the king our master.

Second Sentry

But God said, and it is written: "Thou shalt not kill". Mayhap, if I were to take my sword and cast it from me, I should serve God better than by slaying an enemy.

First Sentry

But it is likewise written: "Eye for eye, tooth for tooth".

Second Sentry

[Sighs] Many things are written. Who can understand them all?

First Sentry

This is idle dreaming. The Chaldeans have invested our town; they wish to burn our houses; I stand here with sword and spear, and will do my utmost to prevent them. Too much knowledge is unwholesome. I know all I want to know.

Second Sentry

Yet I cannot but ask myself ...

First Sentry

[Stubbornly] You should not ask so many questions. A soldier's business is to fight, not to reason why. You ponder overmuch, instead of doing your duty unquestioningly.

Second Sentry

How can a man help questioning himself? How can he be other than uneasy, at such an hour? Do I know where I am, or how long I have still to stand on guard? This darkness beneath the wall, where the masonry is crumbling, will perhaps be my grave to-morrow. Maybe the wind which now caresses my cheek will not find me here in the morning. But can I fail, while I live, to ask the meaning of life? The flame flickers until the torch goes out. How can life do other than question until it is quenched by death? Maybe death is already within me; perchance the questioner is no longer life, but death.

First Sentry

You brood and brood. You are only tormenting yourself to no purpose.

Second Sentry

God has given us a heart precisely that it may torment us.

First Sentry

What is the use of talking about it? We are on guard here. That's enough for me.

Second Sentry

Talking helps to keep us awake, and only the stars hear our words.

[Both are again silent for a time]

Second Sentry

Who goes there? Someone is moving in the darkness.

First Sentry

More busybodies. Why cannot they stay in bed? Send them home.

Second Sentry

No! Let them talk while we stay in the shadow.

First Sentry

You are a strange fellow. I shall continue my round.

[The two sentries pass into the shadow of the tower on the wall, their figures disappearing in the darkness. The gleam of their spears is still seen from time to time.—Jeremiah and Baruch ascend out of the darkness of the stairway and advance to the battlements, Jeremiah hastening on in front, while Baruch, who does not share the prophet's excitement, lags in the rear. The second sentry stands unnoticed in the shadow of the tower]

76

Baruch

Whither are you leading me, master?

Jeremiah

On, on! I must look Terror in the face. [He gazes down into the valley, standing motionless and silent]

Baruch

What are you staring at?

Jeremiah

[Still gazing] The king has come, the king from the north. [He seizes Baruch's sleeve] Come closer, Baruch! Touch my hand that I may know whether I wake or sleep. Are my eyes open? Is this wall builded of stones or of tears? Does Jerusalem lie behind us unheeding in the darkness? Are the forces of Ashur couched in the plain beneath? Tell me, Baruch, convince me that I am dreaming. Shake me till I awake, to laugh at my mad fancy that Zion is encircled by the Chaldeans.

Baruch

What do you mean, master? I don't understand. How can you doubt?

Jeremiah

Alas, it is true, then. I am not dreaming now. The horses are there and the chariots; Ashur is arrayed against Zion; the vision is fulfilled. All these miseries spring from my dreams, for they existed in me before they were in the world of reality. I alone knew, before ever God's words became deeds. In me they arose; through me they came. Yet naught can I do to hinder their flow; nor by sword nor by shield can I stay their progress.

Baruch

Master, you talk at random. Speak in words that I can believe and understand.

Jeremiah

Words that you can believe? But Baruch will you believe the words that I have to say to you at this hour beneath the stars? I fear you will deny me, will laugh at me, for what I would fain say will sound like nonsense in your ears.

Baruch

Faith in you is my very life.

Jeremiah

Hearken, then. [He speaks low and impressively] All that is now happening, I have beheld in my dreams for months past. Not a star shines in heaven which I have not seen above this wall and above God's temple. I have looked down upon the multitude of the foe, upon their myriad tents. Baruch, do you hear me?

Baruch

[Shuddering] I hear, I hear.

Jeremiah

Why was all this made plain to me before the day? It cannot be against God's will that he should disclose his plans to me, should vouchsafe me visions of the future. Nor can I rebel; nor can I be silent; though in truth for long I refused the summons, and stopped my ears to the call. But now, when I see in the real world what has again and again been revealed to me in dreams, for the first time do I feel assured that God speaks through me. I say to you, Baruch, that I am the chosen of the Lord. Woe unto me should I conceal my forebodings from the people and from the king. For this is no more than the beginning, and I know the end.

Baruch

Reveal it, chosen one. Cry your words aloud.

Jeremiah

Baruch, do you see the camp and the tents; do you see this sleeping ocean surging down from the north?

Baruch

[Shuddering] I see the enemy; I see the tents.

Jeremiah

You see the night, sleep, and the false quiet of repose. But in my ears the trumpets blare and the arms clash as the Chaldeans arise and storm the city. The walls whereon our feet are now planted, crumble at their onslaught; the cries of the fugitives ring in my ears. The brazen flood foams over us. I hear the beating of Death's wings o'er city and walls; I see the destruction of Zion. Baruch, waking I see it, for God hath opened an eye within the darkness of my body; my heart maketh a noise in me; my soul hath heard the sound of the trumpet, the alarm of war. Why sleep they still? Time is it they should wake, ere their sleep pass into death. Verily the hour is come to awaken Jerusalem!

Baruch

[Stirred by his words] Yea, yea, Jeremiah, awaken Jerusalem!

Jeremiah

[More and more carried away]
O foolish people, afflicted town,
How, ah how, can you sleep at peace
When Death's cold winding sheet is spread
Beneath you where you lie.
O foolish people, afflicted town,
How can you rest when thunder rages?
How can you drowse,
Lost in dreams,
When Ashur's rams
Are battering the gates?
Who shall waken the fools? Who make the deaf hear?

Baruch

[Ecstatically] You, master. Cry aloud. Awaken them. Save them from the jaws of death.

Jeremiah

Awaken, awaken, up and away!
The land is afire, the foe holds the town!
Flee ere his wrath wholly consume you,

Flee from the sword, flee from the flames,
Leave your possessions, abandon your homes,
Gather your households, your women and children;
Ere he can seize you take refuge in flight.
Up and away!
The land is afire, the foe holds the town!
Up and away!

Second Sentry

[Coming forward from the shadows] Who shouts here? You will waken the sleepers.

Jeremiah

Oh that I could awaken them. Up, Jerusalem, awake! City of God, save thyself.

Second Sentry

You are drunk. Go home to sleep.

Baruch

[Stepping between] Touch him not.

Jeremiah

I must not sleep. No one must sleep. I am the watchman. Woe to him who hinders me.

Second Sentry

[Taking him by the shoulder] You must be moonstruck to think yourself watchman. I am the watchman. Away with you.

Baruch

Touch him not, the chosen of the Lord, the prophet.

Second Sentry

[Loosing Jeremiah] Are you Hananiah, the prophet of God?

Baruch

It is Jeremiah the prophet.

Second Sentry

Jeremiah, who leads the people astray? Jeremiah, who cried through the street that Ashur would prevail? Have you come hither to gloat over the fulfilment of your vision? Too soon, faint-heart, too soon; and yet in an apt moment, prophet of evil, to feel the weight of my anger. I will reveal you something.

Baruch

[Struggling with the sentry] Hands off, touch him not.

First Sentry

[Entering hurriedly] The king is coming. Zedekiah goes the rounds. Clear away the people.

Jeremiah

The king! God be praised! His meaning is plain. The Lord sends him to my hand.

First Sentry

Away chatterer, away.

Second Sentry

Down with you. Away. Creep down there and keep quiet, or you shall rue it.

First Sentry

Here comes the king.

[Jeremiah and Baruch are hustled from the wall and disappear into the dark. The two sentries stand at the extreme edge of the ramparts to leave room for the king and his train to pass. When Zedekiah enters they clash spears on shields in salute and then stand to attention. Zedekiah is making the rounds, accompanied by Abimelech and others. He is unarmed and bareheaded; his face looks pale and thoughtful in the moonlight. He halts, and gazes for a time over the plain]

Zedekiah

See how the camp fires burn athwart the plain. It looks as if the black heavens had fallen upon earth, whence star after star now shines forth. A people countless in numbers is encamped round Israel. Spears are leveled; hands are raised; even in sleep, their dreams turn against us. To-morrow they will all arise as the herbage rises after rain; stillness will be replaced by the screams of death. This is perchance the last night of peaceful slumber.

Abimelech

Be not despondent, O king. Upon this very wall where now thou standest sorely troubled, stood aforetime King Hezekiah. His mind, likewise, was full of care, for in the plain beneath, wave upon wave, countless like these, lay the hosts of Senaccherib. Then, as now, the flood of Ashur threatened the holy city. But the Lord stretched forth his hand and smote the enemy with a pestilence. These walls shall never be broken. Jerusalem endureth for ever.

The Others

Jerusalem endureth for ever.

The Voice of Jeremiah

[From the darkness] Awaken, doomed city, that thou mayest save thyself. Awaken from your heavy slumbers, heedless ones, lest you be slain in sleep; awaken, for the walls are crumbling, and will crush you; awaken, for Ashur's sword is brandished over your heads.

Zedekiah

[On the alert] Who speaks? Who speaks?

Voices

Who speaks?

The Voice of Jeremiah

The anger of the Lord hath fallen upon the disturbers of the peace. God hath sent the king of the north against Israel, to break her towers, and her pride. Awaken that ye may flee; awaken that ye may save yourselves; for he has come, the slayer of your sons, the ravisher of your daughters, he who will lay your fields waste. Awaken, awaken!

Zedekiah

[Shrinking with alarm, and then recovering himself] Who speaks?

First Sentry

A madman, Lord; he is moonstruck.

Voices

Close his mouth.—Away with him.—He is mad.

Zedekiah

Nay, bring him hither. I wish to see him. I wish to see that he who spoke was a living man. Terrible was the sound of his voice. It seemed to me as if the stones of Jerusalem were uttering lamentations, as if the words issued from the very walls.

[The two sentries hasten away into the darkness]

Abimelech

Suffer not thyself to be misled, Lord. Many in the city have been bought with Chaldean gold.

Others

Heed him not.—Hurl him from the wall.—Hold no converse with a coward.

[Jeremiah and Baruch are brought into the light by the sentries, and Jeremiah is thrust forward to the king]

Second Sentry

This is he who spoke the words of shame. He was railing in like fashion, Lord, just before thou camest.

Zedekiah

There has been talk of one going up and down the city and foretelling disaster to the people. Is this the man?

Voices

It is he.—Jeremiah.—Curses light on him.—He foretells disaster.—Poisons men's hearts.—Bears false witness.

Baruch

Nay, he is God's messenger and utters words of truth. I testify for him.

Voices

Who are you to testify?—You are no more than a boy.—Heed him not.— Such vipers should be crushed.

Zedekiah

Silence. Take the young man away, for I need no testimony.

[Baruch is pushed back into the shadows]

Draw nearer, Jeremiah. Art thou he who leadest Israel astray?

Jeremiah

Israel is verily astray, but not by my leadership.

Zedekiah

I know thy voice. My heart tells me that I have heard thee speak, but never before have I seen thy face. Was it thou who criedst aloud for peace at the portal of the palace?

Jeremiah

Yea, Lord, it was I.

Zedekiah

Many voices assailed my ears in that hour, but when I had returned home at nightfall and lay sleepless on my couch, it was thy call which dinned in my ears.

Jeremiah

God's will was that thou shouldst hearken. Woe unto thee that thou heardest not. Had it been otherwise there would be sleep on thy lids and peace in Israel.

Abimelech

[To Jeremiah] What make you here on the wall at night? Would you go over to the Chaldeans? [To the king] Have him seized, for his behavior is suspicious.

A Voice

His mother is on her deathbed, for his words have broken her heart. But he shuns the house, comes here by night, and would parley with the enemy.

Jeremiah

[In alarm] My mother is dying?

Voices

He is a traitor.—Heed him not.—Cast him into prison.

Zedekiah

Be silent, all. My soul is not so weak that I can be swayed by the words of chatterers. Fear not, Jeremiah, I heard thy voice on the day when we decided upon war. It resounded in my heart, for a word of peace is the word of God. But the past is past. War now rages between Ashur and Israel. Words no longer avail. I cannot stop the war at will.

Jeremiah

Nay, Lord, but thou canst.

Zedekiah

[Wrathfully] How, tell me how? Dost thou not see the foe encompassing the walls? Dost thou not hear the spears clashing? What can I do to stop the war?

Jeremiah

The issue is in thy hands, for thou art the king.

Zedekiah

It is too late to talk of peace.

Jeremiah

It is never too late to talk of peace.

Zedekiah

[Still more angrily] Thy words are the words of folly.

Jeremiah

The shedding of blood digs a trench between the nations. The more deeply we dig it, the harder to stop the bloodshed. Therefore let words go before the sword. Seek audience of Nebuchadnezzar; send him an envoy.

Zedekiah

I seek Nebuchadnezzar, my foe?

Jeremiah

Send envoys, while there is yet time to save Jerusalem.

Zedekiah

Why should I be the one to propose a parley?

Jeremiah

Blessed is he who first holds out his hand for peace. Blessed is the king who spares the blood of his people.

Zedekiah

What if I were to offer my hand, only to find the offer rejected?

Jeremiah

Blessed are they who are rejected for justice' sake, for they are men after God's heart.

Zedekiah

I tell thee that the very children would mock me, and the women would laugh at me in my shame.

Jeremiah

Better to be followed by the laughter of fools than by the tears of widows. Think not of thyself; but of the people, which God hath appointed thee to lead. Do God's will, though fools laugh. Thou hast raised thy head against Ashur. Humble thyself now before him.

Zedekiah

Humble myself?

Jeremiah

Humble thyself, anointed of the Lord, for the sake of Jerusalem. Open the gates, open thy heart, thus only canst thou save the city.

Zedekiah

With the sword will I save Jerusalem, at the hazard of my life, but not of my honor. Thou knowest not what thou askest.

Jeremiah

Of thee I demand the hardest of duties, as is befitting for the Lord's anointed. Offer up thy pride, the treasure of thy heart, for the sake of Jerusalem. Kneel before Nebuchadnezzar, even as I kneel before thee.

Open the gates, and open thy heart. Abase thyself, King Zedekiah, for it is better thou shouldst be abased than that Israel should be laid low.

Zedekiah
Away with thee, away! I will humble myself before no man on earth.

Jeremiah
[Springing impetuously to his feet] Accurst, then, be the oil with which thou wast anointed. Zion has been entrusted to thy hands, and by thy hands is Zion destroyed. Mayst thou be forgotten by God's mercy, even as thou hast forgotten Jerusalem. A curse be upon thee, murderer of Zion.

Abimelech
Throw him from the wall!

Voices
He has slandered the king.—Throw him from the wall.

[The members of the king's train close in on Jeremiah]

Zedekiah
[Who has yielded ground as if attacked by an unseen enemy, recovering himself] Desist! Harm him not. Think ye that the curse of a fool can affright me, or an impudent word unman me? [A pause] Nevertheless, the rumor is true, and this man's speech is full of danger. Like a ram do his words batter at men's hearts. No longer must such a liar speak freely to the people, endeavoring to spread dismay among our warriors.

Abimelech
He should be put to death. Unworthy to live is the man who has lost faith in God.

Voices
Stone the hireling.—He would sell the town to the Chaldeans.—He prays for our defeat.—Slay him.

Zedekiah

Shall I kill the man who slandered me, that it may be said he filled me with fear? Jeremiah, I value thy words lightly as air; but once more, for thine own sake, I ask thee the question. Does thy heart faithfully assure thee that death hangs over Zion and over all within her walls? Speak freely.

Jeremiah

Death is over Jerusalem. Death's hand is upon us all. Naught but surrender can save us.

Zedekiah

Away then, and surrender. Save thine own life.

[Jeremiah stares at him in bewilderment]

No man shall sap our powers while he eats our bread. If thou fearest for Zion, flee from Zion. I give thee thy life. Climb down the wall; seek out Nebuchadnezzar; take shelter in his camp. If thy word be fulfilled, puff out thy cheeks and laugh at thy brethren who died for Jerusalem.

Abimelech

Too gentle, O king, in thy dealings with this slanderer.

[Jeremiah struggles for speech]

Zedekiah

Away, renegade, away! Seek out Nebuchadnezzar, whose victory thou foretellest. Kiss his feet. I stay in the midst of my people and in the home of my fathers, for my faith shall remain steadfast till my last breath. False are this man's words! Jerusalem endureth for ever!

The Others

[Shouting] Jerusalem endureth for ever.—God's house shall never pass away.

Zedekiah

Haste, haste to Ashur. I give thee free permission. Leave us to our deaths; and for thy part, crawl to safety.

Jeremiah

[Controlling himself] I will not forsake Jerusalem.

Zedekiah

Didst thou not even now assure us that death was hanging over Zion? Flee, that thou at least save thyself alive.

Jeremiah

Not for my own life am I filled with sorrow. It is for the life of thousands upon thousands that my heart is heavy. I will not flee. If Zion's walls fall, I will fall with them.

Zedekiah

I have warned thee, Jeremiah, as thou warnedst me. Henceforth thy life is in thine own charge. [To the others] Let none molest him while he keeps due measure. But should he again seek to spread terror, seize and bind him, and he shall pay for it with his life. [To Jeremiah] Guard thyself, place a seal on thy lips, lest thy life atone for speech. May God spare us, as I have spared thee to-day.

Jeremiah

[Motionless, his voice unsteady] Not myself would I guard, but Jerusalem.

Zedekiah

[Returning to the outer edge of the wall] Still they come! Still they come! The noise of their chariot wheels and the trampling of their chargers are like the growling of a storm. Terrible indeed is the king of the north. Dreadful will it be to encounter him. God save Jerusalem! [Breathes deeply] God save Jerusalem.

[Zedekiah turns away, and slowly resumes the round, plunged in thought. He is followed by Abimelech and the other members of the train. The two sentries move after them out of sight]

Baruch

[Rushing forward from the shadow] Quick, quick! Hasten after him. The spirit of God is upon you. Hasten that you may compel him.

Jeremiah

[Awakening as from a trance] Compel whom?

Baruch

The king. Let your words be like flame. Save Jerusalem.

Jeremiah

The king? [He looks round horror-stricken upon the deserted wall] Lost, lost the sacred hour. My hasty tongue has ruined all.

Baruch

Try once again and you will overcome him. Already he was yielding.

Jeremiah

Too late, too late. Why did God choose a weakling? Why did he put words of gall into my mouth?

Baruch

Do not torment yourself, master. Your sufferings confuse your mind.

Jeremiah

Think you so? But I have failed. To whom have I brought joy? I am a horror to the upright and a grievous affliction to my mother. No wife bears my child in her womb, nor does any one living believe in my words.

Baruch

I believe you. I will not forsake you. You are great. I cleave to you for your very sorrow.

Jeremiah

Praise me not. My soul burns with shame. What have I done that shall profit Jerusalem? Have I softened the king's heart; have I led the erring people into the right path; have I found an envoy of peace? How, when I myself have faltered, shall I show the way for an envoy?

Baruch

You seek an envoy from Nebuchadnezzar to our king?

Jeremiah

Will Nebuchadnezzar be readier to parley than Zedekiah? Kings are like boys, each waiting for the other to begin.

Baruch

[Ardently] Jeremiah, your words bear fruit in my soul.

Jeremiah

What mean you?

Baruch

This deed is for me. Well know I that the road leads through the valley of the shadow, even as yours. But I will walk it for the sake of Jerusalem. Master, farewell.

Jeremiah

Whither will you go?

Baruch

Farewell, master. Your blessing should I succeed. Spare me your curse should I fail. For Jerusalem! [He begins to climb down the wall]

Jeremiah

But Baruch, whither are you going?

Baruch

By your road. Farewell. [He disappears over the parapet]

Jeremiah

[Leaning forward] Whither, Baruch, whither? Stay, they will seize you. Already the spies of Chaldea block every road. Baruch, stand by me in this hour. Baruch, Baruch!

First Sentry

[Running in] Who calls there in the night? What is afoot?

Jeremiah

[Standing up] I call, I call; but no one heeds me.

First Sentry

Still you, is it? What are you doing here? I thought I saw a shadow pass down the wall. Are you alone?

Jeremiah

I am alone! I am alone!

[Slowly, with heavy steps, Jeremiah passes towards the town. The sentry stares after him until he is swallowed up in the gloom. Then the soldier resumes his march to and fro in the moonlight. Nothing is heard save his footsteps on the flagstones, until from a distance the challenge: "Samson guard us", "Samson guard us", begins to pass once more round the walls]

THE PROPHET'S ORDEAL

SCENE FIVE

Yet it pleased the Lord to bruise him; he hath put him to grief. Isaiah LIII, 10.

SCENE FIVE

The small bed-chamber where Jeremiah's Mother lies ill. Doorways and windows are covered with curtains to exclude light and sound. The interior is so dark that the figures of those in the chamber are barely visible. The white bed-furniture is conspicuous in the gloom. Close to the bed stands Ahab, the elderly servingman.

Jochebed
[A female relative, coming from without, cautiously draws aside the curtain over the doorway] Ahab!

Ahab
Speak low! Tread softly! Her sleep is light as thistle-down. A breath will scatter it.

Jochebed
Well for one who can still sleep, when the gates of the city are being assailed.

Ahab
Not a word of the matter. Not a word of the enemy. As you love her, spare her.

Jochebed
What do you mean? What must I not speak of?

Ahab
Not a word of our troubles. She knows naught of Jerusalem's evil plight.

Jochebed
I don't understand. She does not know that the town is besieged?

Ahab
Why should we tell her what is impending? The very thought would kill her.

Jochebed

[Greatly astonished] She does not know that Ashur is upon us? Is there still a living being within the walls who remains ignorant of our misery? How has this miracle been wrought? Are her senses closed? Is she deaf to the hosannas? Does she think we are at peace when the battering rams thunder against the walls?

Ahab

Her senses are dulled. Such noises as she hears seem the noises of a dream. I have closed the entries, shutting out sound and light.

Jochebed

She knows nothing? Wonderful, and yet horrible. Has she no suspicion?

Ahab

At times she has suspected, but I have been able to calm her fears. Yesterday, when the first rams were at work, she was alarmed by the cries of the populace. Throwing off the coverlet, she wrung her hands, and declared she must forth to the walls, that war had come, that the enemy was in the city, that Zion was perishing. Her son's prophecy was being fulfilled, the king of the north had come. She struggled to her feet. Then her knees gave way beneath her. I caught her as she fell, bore her back to bed, and persuaded her that it was all a dream, that the shouting and the hosannas were but the illusion of fever. She seemed to believe me, lying with open eyes, and listening to the muffled clamor from the street.

Jochebed

'Tis wondrous strange. But what has thus confused her?

Ahab

In her sickness she craves for her son.

Jochebed

Jeremiah, the madman! The zealot of the streets. She herself drove him from the house.

Ahab

Not for an hour since has she known happiness. She sat ever in silence, or stood at the door like one awaiting a guest. When he failed to return, her mind gradually became confused.

Jochebed

Why then comes he not, the reprobate, that he may restore her to health? He tramps the streets spewing curses among the people, while his mother is dying for lack of him. Why comes he not, chatterer in the market, slayer of peace?

Ahab

He knows naught of her longing. No less proud is he than she, and he will never cross the threshold until he is summoned.

Jochebed

Summon him then.

Ahab

How dare I without her command? I am but a servingman. How can I act upon words which she mutters unwitting?

Jochebed

You may and you must, since her life is at stake.

Ahab

Do you believe I should do rightly to summon Jeremiah without awaiting her command?

Jochebed

By God's mercy I believe it. Thus will you save her alive.

Ahab

God be praised, Jochebed. In my sore need I have already done what you wish.

Jochebed

A blessing on you therefor!

Ahab

I have sent my boys seeking him.

Jochebed

If they can but find him. Lacking him, she will die of mingled pride and longing.

Ahab

Truly, since she drove him forth, she has been unceasingly at war with herself.

Jochebed

Who is at peace in this stormy time?

[The mother wakens with a sigh]

Jochebed

[Speaking softly to Ahab] Ahab, she stirs, she is waking. Her eyes are still closed, but her lips move as if to speak.

[Ahab bends over the sick woman]

The Mother

[Speaks with closed eyes, the tones of her voice like those of a song heard in the distance] Has he come? Is he here? Where is he, the son of my sorrow?

Jochebed

[Whispering] How wonderful! For the first time she speaks of him plainly.

Ahab

Nay, she is still dreaming.

The Mother

[Moves and opens her eyes] Are you there, Ahab? Is that you Jochebed? My dreams are dark and uneasy.

Ahab

[Tenderly] How do you feel? Have you slept well?

The Mother

How can I sleep well, when my dreams are so dreadful? Where is he? I saw him. Why did he go away?

Ahab

Whom do you mean?

The Mother

Why did he go away? Why did you let him go away?

Ahab

There has been no one in the room but Jochebed and me.

The Mother

Not he? Not he? The house is haunted with dreams. [She sits up suddenly in bed, glancing round with feverish anxiety] Why do you not summon him?

Ahab

Summon whom?

The Mother

How can you ask? Can you not see that death's hand is upon me? Yet you will not send for him.

Ahab

How should I dare ...

The Mother

Alas, that I should be immured here, too ill to move, tended by blind servants with hearts of stone. Away, away.

Ahab

But mistress ...

The Mother

You have betrayed me. You have forbidden him the house. I know he must have come, and you have barred the door. He has been here. My instinct tells me. He waits but the summons, and you will not send. You have denied him entry.

Ahab

Hearken, mistress ...

The Mother

Woe is me! Away! May you die as I am dying, abandoned by your children; may you die in the straw like an outcast.

Ahab

Let me say a word ...

The Mother

One word only will I listen to, that he is coming, that he is here.

Ahab

That is what I would fain tell you. He is coming. His footsteps draw nigh.

The Mother

[Rapturously] He is coming, my Jeremiah? Deceive me not, Ahab. Cheat not a dying woman.

Jochebed

Ahab has already sent his sons to seek out Jeremiah.

The Mother

He is coming. Is it true? Yes, I hear him. I hear his footfall. I hear him in the house. He knocks at the door, knocks within my heart. Hasten, man, hasten. Why do you tarry to admit him?

Ahab

[Endeavoring to calm her] Mistress, he will be here anon. Early this morning did I send my boys.

The Mother

[In excitement once more] Nay, he will not come. Your lads are slothful, and are idling in the streets. Would they but hasten. The darkness gains on me. If I could but see him ere I sink into it. Run, Ahab, he may be at the door.

Ahab

Have patience, you will do yourself a harm.

The Mother

Why do you not let him in? Can you not hear how he is hammering at the door? I feel it in my temples. Open to him, open.

Ahab

Not yet is he here, but he will come ere long.

Jochebed

He will soon be here. Have patience a while.

The Mother

No, no; he is there, but you are keeping him from me. My time is short. My limbs are cold ...

[Jeremiah comes quietly into the doorway, and remains standing in doubt, his hands clenched, his head bowed as if he were carrying a heavy burden]

Ahab

Don't throw yourself about so. He will be here anon.

[Catching sight of Jeremiah, he starts and stops speaking. Jochebed likewise preserves an anxious silence. For a few moments no one speaks in the darkened room]

The Mother

[Raising herself with difficulty] Why are you both silent? [She suddenly gives a cry of joy] Has he come? Is my Jeremiah here? Where are you, Jeremiah?

[Hesitatingly, Jeremiah moves forward a few steps. He, too, is a prey to strong emotion]

The Mother

[Stretching out her arms towards him] You are there, I feel it. Would that I could see you clearly. Why come you not close, that I may touch you?

Jeremiah

[Not moving, his hands still clenched] I dare not, I dare not. Disaster dogs my footsteps. Curses go before me. Let me stand thus apart, lest my breath harm you, lest it strike terror to your soul.

The Mother

[Feverishly] My child, my arms crave for you. Come close, dear, come close. Are my lips so hateful to you? Is my hand so estranged?

Jeremiah

I am estranged from myself, and a stranger in this house.

The Mother

Alas, he repels me, will leave me once more. What makes you so cold, so hard-hearted?

Jeremiah

A word burns between us like the sword of the angel of God.

The Mother

The curse, for which I have cursed myself a thousand times? Idle breath was it, and the wind has blown it away.

Jeremiah

Nay, Mother, the curse stands, and all the streets are filled with it. It rebounds from the wall of every house, attacks me from all men's mouths. No longer am I your son, no longer living flesh, but the mock of the world, an outcast from my people, hated by the righteous, forgotten by God, loathed by myself. To myself leave me. Let me remain in the darkness, most accurst of all men.

The Mother

My child, were you indeed the rejected of all men, banned by the priests, outlawed by the people; had God himself thrust you away from the light of his countenance; still were you my son, blood of my blood for evermore. I will love you for their hatred, and bless you for their curse. If they have spit upon you, come that I may kiss you; if they have cast you out, come that I may take you in; home, come home to my heart. Sweet to me is the bitterness of your lips, sweet the salt of your tears; blessed is all that you do; if only you return to my mother's heart.

Jeremiah

[Falling to his knees with a groan] Mother, spirit of eternal kindness. Mother, you give me back my lost world.

[The mother folds him in her arms, and clasps him without speaking for a time. Tremblingly she strokes his head and his body again and again. At length, as she looks at him, a strange glow of happiness lights up her face, and she speaks to him in a plaintive chant]

The Mother

Child of my heart, whom the world thrusts aloof,
Had you but stayed with me, ne'er left my roof!
Home now returning, find peace in my arms,
They hold you once more, son, safe from all harms.

Tranquilly cradled, unscathed shall you bide,
Keeping the house, no more ranging wide.
Tenderly stroking your brow and your hair,
I will set your heart free from all sorrow and care,
And the curse which I spoke on that ill-omened day,
Lo, with my hands I have brushed it away!

Jeremiah

[Awestruck] Oh Mother, how thin your hands have become;
Oh Mother, how wan your cheeks have become.
Your heart is scarce beating; your lips are so pale.
How can I help you? Can nothing avail?

The Mother

My days have been lonely, my nights have been dreary.
When you did not return, I grew heart-sick and weary.
Your absence was killing me. Now you are back,
Your coming suffices. Naught more do I lack.

Jeremiah

Through the streets did I wander, my heart turned to stone.
Your forgiveness now craving, I fain would atone.

The Mother

Nightly I dreamed your dreams,
As I lay in the empty house,
Alone and forsaken.
By day they lurked in the shadows;
But as night fell,
Stealing forth from dark corners,
Like toads, bats, and owls,
They crawled and flittered round my temples,
Filling my soul with horror.
Rending and gnawing,
Devouring sleep,
Like vampires did they sap my strength,
So that the dawning of day

Found me hag-ridden,
Shattered and broken.
Jeremiah, I adjure you,
Leave me not again.
Jeremiah, I implore you,
Stay with me, stay with me,
For the time is short.

Jeremiah
Mother, what mean you?

The Mother
Seek not to deceive me.
Think you I know not
That death draws near?
Even as on a dial
The shadow rises
Stage by stage up the wall
While the sun sinks in the west,
So, with every breath I draw,
Does darkness rise within me.
Woe is me that, still living and aware,
I feel the grip of death's cold hand.

Jeremiah
Nay, Mother, God's purpose with us is plain.
How can you think he will part us anew?
No more am I froward. Your child once again,
I am sent back by him for a fresh life with you.
Were it otherwise, say to me why should I be
Unclouded by visions, from dreaming set free?

The Mother
Do you dream no longer?

Jeremiah
My sleep is dreamless; my slumber is mute.

The night-time faces trouble me no more.
My dreams have become daylight realities.
Revealed in full horror, they stalk 'neath the sun.
I dream no longer, now the world's awake.

The Mother

[Ecstatically, for she has heeded only the first part of Jeremiah's speech]
Your dreaming is over?
Then joy comes again.
Indeed, I was certain
That God in his mercy
Would scatter the darkness
That clouded your brain.
Recall but my words
When we parted in pain:
Ne'er shall an enemy circle our wall,
David's city be taken, Jerusalem fall.
Though foes from the ends of the earth should rage,
The towering battlements ever shall stand.
Firm Israel's heart, and mighty her hand,
Eternal the days of Jerusalem.

Jeremiah

[Rises from his knees. He stares blankly as he mutters in amaze]
Ne'er shall ... an enemy ... circle ... our wall?

The Mother
What sudden fear assails your soul?
What thought steals color from your cheek?

Jeremiah
[Still shuddering]
Ne'er shall ... an enemy ... circle ... our wall?

The Mother

Jeremiah,
What has befallen you?
What has frightened you?
What has taken you aback?
And you,
Ahab and Jochebed,
Why are you making signs to him?
Jeremiah, I conjure you,
Tell me what is amiss.

Jeremiah

There is nothing wrong, Mother, nothing at all.
I was but mazed for a moment,
Startled out of myself by your words.

The Mother

Nay, nay, it is false.
Your faces, of a sudden, grew dark and careworn;
Now you all turn away, exchange glances, and whisper.
Awesome, indeed, must be the secret you hide.
It chills me like death;
Like God's wrath it affrights me.

Jeremiah

[Stammering] Nothing, Mother, we are hiding nothing.

The Mother

Why seek to deceive me? Why hoodwink my eyes?
Not yet am I dead, nor in coffin enclosed.
Life's breath in my lungs,
Life's pulse at my heart,
I can hear, I can speak;
Why then hide ye the truth?

Jeremiah

Mother, you are distraught with fever. Your temples are burning, your hands are cold.

The Mother

Why are doors and windows curtained so close?
Why is all so dark and still?
You stifle me in wrappings,
Bury me in cushions,
Me, who am yet alive.
Tell me, tell me why.

Jeremiah

Mother, calm yourself. Take my hands. I am here beside you.

The Mother

I live, I live; I say to you that I live.
No longer shall you deceive me.
Fearful is my awakening.
Too well do I know the truth,
That my dreams were not dreams but realities.
Again and again did I hear
The rolling of the chariots,
The trampling of the chargers,
The clashing of the weapons,
The singing of the hosannas.
Muffled were the sounds,
As they reached me in this darkened room;
And I fancied all was a dream.
Yet now I am awake,
Horribly awake.
Death has forced open my lids.
I know
Why you have shut away light and sound.
Disaster assails the city, has entered the gates.
We are besieged, we are lost.
Woe is me, there is war in Israel!

Jeremiah

Mother, Mother!

The Mother

Jeremiah, speak!
Tell me,
Is he come,
He whose advent you foretold,
The king of kings from the north?

Jeremiah

Mother, you are dreaming.

Jochebed

[Whispering] Lie to her! For her life's sake, lie to her!

The Mother

[In delirium]
Alas, hear the trumpets
Sounding the onslaught!
He comes in his panoply,
The king from the north.
War is upon us.
They swarm to attack.
The ramparts are crumbling,
The gates broken down.
The city is lost,
The temple destroyed.
I am crushed in the ruins,
I burn in my bed.
Save me, oh save me,
Jeremiah, save me,
Carry me forth!

Jeremiah

[Kneels beside her]
Mother, an evil fancy
Enthrals your mind.
Mother, hearken.

The Mother

I hold your hands.
Swear to me, swear,
That it is not true.
Swear to me, swear,
That no danger threatens Israel.
Swear to me, swear,
That no enemy shall disturb my last rest,
That my burial place shall be Zion.

Jeremiah

So shall it be. God will be gracious to us in death as in life.

The Mother

Jeremiah,
Do I wander in mind?
Is the foe at the gates?
Or is our world filled with peace?

[Jeremiah struggles vainly for words]

Ahab

[Breaking in on his hesitation]
Deceive her, speak ere she passes.
Can you not see
How the darkness shadows her face,
As the angel of death hovers nigh?
Speak, and chase the terror from her soul.

Jochebed
Speak, or it will be too late.
A word, only one word,
So that she may die in peace.

Jeremiah
[Still struggling with contending passions]
I cannot, I cannot.
There is one grips my throat,
Holds my soul in his grasp.

The Mother
He is silent.
It must then be true
That God has smitten his own people:
May the day perish wherein I was born!
Alas, the darkness gains on me.
Fire ravages the land.
I burn. Bear me forth.

Ahab
[Interrupting, to Jeremiah] A word, only one word.

Jeremiah
[Choking, as if strangled]
No such word can I utter.
God's hand grips my throat;
God's hand grasps my soul.
Ah, cruel one, free me ...

The Mother
[With a wild cry]
Lost, all is lost.
I burn.
The city ... the temple ... God falls.
God has fallen!
The flames of Gehenna strike home to my heart.

Jerusalem!

[She collapses suddenly. There is silence]

[Ahab and Jochebed move in alarm to the bedside and bend over the dead woman]

Jeremiah
[His voice bursting forth as when a fountain is unsealed]
It is false!
I lied, I lied!
Eternal the days of Jerusalem.
Ne'er shall an enemy circle our wall,
David's city be taken, Jerusalem fall.
O Mother, once again give ear.
I swear it, look you, I solemnly swear,
Eternal the days of Jerusalem!

Ahab
[Fiercely]
Away!
Your oaths will not waken her!
Leave her in peace!

Jeremiah
She must hear me before 'tis too late.

Ahab
[Bitterly] As you say, 'tis too late.
Away from the room.
Your cries will not waken her,
Nor your lies break her sleep.
While she lived you were silent,
Unfeeling as stone.
Idle dreamer and outcast,
Hence, get you begone!

Jochebed
Away, rejected of men,
Scorn of the just,
Away from the house.
Why, ah why,
Did she readmit you?
Away, man accurst,
Break not the calm
Of the death which you wrought.

Jeremiah
[Overwhelmed]
Ever accursèd,
Ever rejected,
Thrust forth from home,
Unfriended to roam.
God, God, it is hard to bear men thy word!

[Ahab and Jochebed pay the last duties to the dead, pressing down the eyelids, and wrapping the body in a shroud. Ahab goes to the pitchers and sprinkles water on the ground. No sound but their solemn paces can be heard. Jeremiah stares before him in stupor. Silence prevails for a time, full of the mystery of death. Then a clamor is heard without. There is a vehement knocking at the door]

Ahab
Who knocks?

Jochebed
There is a turbulent crowd without.

Ahab
They assail the door as if they were enemies. You had better open.

Jochebed
Hark to the savages, they have burst in the door.

114

[The sound of splintering wood is heard. Then hasty footsteps. Zebulon, Pashur, Hananiah, the First Sentry, and many others, rush in]

Zebulon
He must be here.

A Boy
I saw him go in.

Voices
So did I.—He slipped in an hour back.—I was on watch as you ordered.—I saw him too.

Ahab
Whom do you seek?

Pashur
Deliver him up—the man you are hiding.

Zebulon
We will have blood for blood.

Ahab
What mean ye by breaking in here? Away, rabble.

Pashur
[Catching sight of the corpse, raises his hands and speaks reverently] Praise to the eternal judge. May he be merciful to the just. [Turning away he passes into the background]

The Others
[Suddenly stilled, murmur] Praise to the eternal judge.

One Speaks
[Gently] Who has died?

Ahab

One from whom God had hidden the light of his countenance. One full of sorrows, and acquainted with grief. One whose bitterest affliction was that she gave birth to the enemy of her nation.

Another Speaks

Jeremiah!

Zebulon

It is Jeremiah whom we seek. Where is Jeremiah?

Jeremiah

[Comes forward, speaking loudly in grief and indignation] Who seeks Jeremiah? Who still desires to rain curses on me? Let him come, let him curse. I am the mark for all the curses in the world.

Zebulon

It is I, wretch, who come to curse you, I, Zebulon, father of Baruch, whom you have led astray. Where is my son?

Jeremiah

[Tonelessly] How should I know? Am I your son's keeper?

Hananiah

This man makes a charge against you. Answer, Jeremiah.

Jeremiah

He, too, makes a charge. Should I begin to bring charges I should speak from now till midnight.

Voices

He answers not.—He talks at random, evading the charge.—Pashur, Hananiah, make an end.—Pass judgment upon him.

Hananiah

Have you brought witnesses, Zebulon?

Zebulon

My son has vanished from the town. He has been continually with Jeremiah. On the ramparts, last night, this man heard Jeremiah inciting Baruch to desert to the enemy.

Hananiah

[To the First Sentry] Do you bear this witness?

First Sentry

Verily, prophet, while I stood on guard, there came two men. One was Jeremiah, well known to me. The other was young, little more than a boy, with black hair and flashing eyes.

Zebulon

It was Baruch my son, whom this man hath corrupted.

First Sentry

There was much talk between them. Jeremiah prophesied disaster, so that my heart grew hot within me.

Hananiah

[To the others] Do you hear? He prophesied the fall of Zion.

First Sentry

When the king had gone, and Jeremiah and the other were alone, then the other, he whom you name Baruch, climbed down the wall and deserted to the enemy, leaving Jeremiah on the ramparts.

Zebulon

Do you hear, men of Israel? I charge Jeremiah with leading my son astray, with bringing shame upon my house.

Pashur

[Advancing to the front] Your answer, Jeremiah. What say you to this charge? [Jeremiah is silent] Do you call witnesses?

Jeremiah

[In low tones] The one who would testify for me must not be named.

Pashur

Will he come forward in due time?

[Jeremiah is silent]

Voices

Make an end, make an end.

Pashur

Silence. I will hold just judgment! Jeremiah, I cite you to answer. [Jeremiah is silent] You are charged with having, in defiance of the king's command, foretold disaster.

[Jeremiah is silent]

Hananiah

Do you deny your words? [Jeremiah still holds his peace] Lo, the fear of death has moved him at length. For the first time he is silent.

Jeremiah

You who have misled Israel, would you tempt me to say No when God says Yes, and Yes when God says No? More strongly hath he tempted me to depart from his ways, yet would I not depart from them. He raised up one against me whose breath was dearer to me than the breath of my own life, but I would not yield to her, for the Lord cuts from the tree of life him whom he hath chosen for a scourge. Go, and leave me in peace.

Zebulon

I will not go. He has destroyed my son. I demand judgment.

118

Pashur

Twice have I charged you to speak. You have spoken when you should have been silent; now you are silent when you should speak. For the third time I cite you. [Jeremiah is silent] Hear then my judgment. No longer shall you seek to daunt the courageous, no longer shall you lead youth astray, Jeremiah, the son of Hilkiah in Israel.

Jeremiah

Make short work! Wither me no longer with your glances. Enough, enough.

Pashur

You shall be lowered into a pit, that you may no longer be an offence to God's daylight, nor your voice an affliction to the city. May you perish, and your words with you, in the darkness of the earth.

Jeremiah

Life is affliction! Words are affliction! Blessed be darkness, thrice blessed the tomb.

Pashur

Lay hands on him. Execute judgment!

Voices

Oh, just judgment!—Great is the wisdom of Pashur.—Away with Jeremiah. —Fetch a rope, that we may lower him into the pit.

Jeremiah

[Shrinking from their touch] Touch me not. Better, far better is darkness, for the hour is at hand in Israel when the living will envy the dead, and when those that wake will envy the sleepers. My heart yearns for silence; my soul is consumed with longing that I may become brother to the dead. Make way, I will bury myself, that I may deliver myself from the world, and Israel of my presence. [He folds his arms and moves towards the doorway. The others begin to follow him hesitatingly]

Hananiah

[Bursting in on the silence with an exultant cry] Rejoice, Zion, for broken is the song of thy destruction, rent are the lips of thy slanderer. Rejoice, Zion, for eternal is thy springtime. Jerusalem endureth for ever!

[Jeremiah turns fiercely, raising his arms as if about to rebuke Hananiah. His eyes flash fire. Those at his heels draw back in alarm, as from a wild beast at bay. But Jeremiah controls himself. His arms sink to his sides, and the fierce expression vanishes from his countenance. With a last look at the dead form of his mother, he regains composure. Covering his face, he walks forth alone, like one carrying a heavy burden. The rest follow in disorder. Last of all walks Pashur, deep in thought. Ahab and Jochebed are left, looking at one another uneasily. Ahab takes a linen sheet and spreads it reverently over the body]

VOICES IN THE NIGHT

SCENE SIX

Evening cometh and the shadows lengthen. Jeremiah, VI, 4.

SCENE SIX

King Zedekiah's bed-chamber, large and stately. It is dimly lighted, so that details are scarcely visible. What light there is comes from a lamp hanging in a golden bowl, and from the soft moonbeams which stream in through the casement. This is widely open and commands a view of the town. In the foreground stands a large table surrounded by broad seats. The curtained bed occupies the center of the background. Zedekiah is standing motionless at the window, looking down on the moonlit city. Joab, a young spearman, enters, and stands respectfully waiting for the king to notice him. Zedekiah pays no heed, but continues to gaze out of the window.

The Lad
[After a pause ventures to speak] My Lord King! [Zedekiah turns with a start] It is midnight, O King. This is the hour at which thou orderedst me to summon the council.

Zedekiah
Are they all here?

The Lad
All, at thy command.

Zedekiah
Have they come unseen by the people and by the palace servants?

The Lad
Unseen, Lord King. By secret ways I led them hither.

Zedekiah
Where is the spy? Hast thou kept him apart?

The Lad
He tarries with the doorkeepers.

Zedekiah
Let him tarry. Summon the council.

[The Lad bows, and disappears through the doorway]

Zedekiah
[Strides to and fro, and then returns to the window. He soliloquizes]
Never have I seen the stars shine so brightly. They stand confusedly in
rows, like letters on the dark background of heaven, a writing which no
man can read. In Babylon, they say, are interpreters and priests who
serve the stars, conversing with them by night. Other kings can talk with
their gods; they have shrines on their towers where they can learn the
will of heaven when their hearts are troubled. Why have I no soothsayers
who can tell the future? It is terrible to be the servant of a god who is
always silent; whom no one has ever seen! [A pause while he
contemplates the city] They are all asleep, those over whom I rule; they
rest beside their wives or beside their weapons; in me is centered their
need and their wakefulness. I must counsel others, but who shall counsel
me? I must lead others, but who shall lead me? I am exalted over others,
but over me is exalted one whom I cannot see. Below is sleep; above is
silence.

[The Lad draws aside the curtain; and the five councilors enter
noiselessly. They are Pashur, the high priest; Hananiah, the prophet;
Imre, the oldest burgher; Abimelech, the general; Nahum, the steward.
Zedekiah turns to receive them. They bow]

Zedekiah
I summoned you by night that our talk might be private. I demand from
you a pledge of secrecy. Lay your hands within the priest's hands; he will
answer for you to the Most High. [Silently they raise their hands in
adjuration, and each in turn lays his hand in Pashur's] I swear by
Almighty God that I will show no anger against any who opposes me. [He
lays his hand in Pashur's] Now let us take counsel. [He waves them
towards the table, and all take their seats] We are in the eleventh month
of the siege. The vines are green once more. Nebuchadnezzar has been
unable to take Jerusalem, but we on our part have not been able to force
him to raise the siege. His sword against us beats the water, but so
likewise does ours beat the water against him. We have left nothing

undone that might bring aid. I have sent envoys to the king of the Medes; I have sent to the princes of the east, asking their help against Ashur. The missions were fruitless. We stand alone.

Hananiah

[Fiercely] God is on our side.

[The others say nothing]

Zedekiah

[Quietly] God is on our side. He has set up his tabernacle upon this hill, and my own roof stands in the shadow of his holy house. But God sends trials upon his own people. Those who swore faith to us, betrayed us; the Egyptians abandoned us; we are alone. Let us take counsel together, how to fight out our quarrel with Nebuchadnezzar, or whether we can find a means to end it.

Hananiah

Let us pray to God for a miracle. Let our hearts overflow with prayer, our altars smoke with sacrifices. What we have done once hitherto, let us now do twice over.

Nahum

There is nothing left to sacrifice, neither bulls nor rams.

Hananiah

It is false. I have heard the lowing of the cattle which you refuse to deliver up to the sacrifice.

Nahum

The last we have. They are milch cows to provide food for nursing mothers and the sick.

Hananiah

Such thrift is impious where God is concerned. Let the sick starve and the breasts of the women run dry, so long as God receives due meed of sacrifice.

124

Pashur

[Earnestly] God requires no gifts to make him aware of our distresses.

Hananiah

Naught is sweeter to the Lord than the gifts of the needy. We should give to the uttermost, tearing the morsels from our own mouths.

Pashur

I know the customs. It is not for you, Hananiah, to teach me my duty, which I know better perchance than you know God's word and God's will.

Hananiah

Who sacrifices grudgingly, who sacrifices with a cold heart, is but a slaughterman, and no true servant of the Lord. Lo, I say unto you unless ye give of your uttermost need, ye are unworthy to stand in the light of his countenance.

Zedekiah

[Passionately] Hold your peace. Your words are past bearing. But a few grains of sand have run through the hour glass, and already you rail against one another. We do not meet to discuss what it is fitting we should render unto God. We meet to consider our pressing need, and how we can relieve it. We are in the throes of war, and to you therefore I turn first for counsel, Abimelech, general of my army.

Abimelech

Stout are the walls of Jerusalem, O King, but stouter still is my heart.

Zedekiah

And your men, old stalwart; are they, too, stout-hearted? Rarely do I hear them raise exultant cries. When I pass among them, no longer do they strike their shields. They turn away their faces.

Abimelech

War makes men silent, but it steels their hearts. No longer, indeed, do they shout with delight, for that they can use their swords freely. Custom stales all joys. But they watch and wait; strong as brass are they, guarding the walls of Jerusalem.

Zedekiah
But what if the moons still wax and wane; what if the second year of the siege begins? There is no help coming from outside.

Abimelech
The siege will last as long as God pleases, and we shall last as long as the siege.

Zedekiah
May the Lord fulfil thy words. [To the others] Are ye all of the same opinion?

Pashur
We must be steadfast, enduring patiently until the end.

Zedekiah
What sayest thou, Hananiah?

Hananiah
Never shall Nebuchadnezzar overthrow us. Woe unto all faint-hearts. Did it rest with me, I would put them to the sword.

Imre
Mine eyes are dim with age, but being old, I saw the days when Senaccherib was arrayed against Israel, and I saw his men lying dead in heaps around our walls. Never were the jackals so fat as in the year when Jerusalem was encircled by the enemies of the Lord. The same may happen again to those who now besiege us. Let mine eyes not be wholly darkened ere this day dawn. Jerusalem endureth for ever!

Abimelech, Hananiah, Pashur
Jerusalem endureth for ever!

[A pause]

Zedekiah
Thou sayest nothing, Nahum. Wherefore art thou silent?

Nahum
Gloomy are my thoughts, Lord King, and bitter will be my speech. He thrusts not himself forward, to whom joy is lacking.

Zedekiah
I summoned you in council, one and all. Welcome is the bearer of good tidings, but no less welcome he who brings wise warnings. Speak freely.

Nahum
Shortly before you called me to the council, I was visiting the storehouses, and having the grain measured, bushel by bushel. They were full when the siege began, but now they are almost empty. No longer can we provide a whole loaf for the day's ration.

[All sit in dismayed silence]

Zedekiah
Was there not ample provision of grain from the villages? Was not an abundance of milch cows and other beasts driven within the walls?

Nahum
Forget not that the siege has lasted nearly a year, and that there are many mouths to feed.

Zedekiah
[After another pause] We can reduce the rations yet further. Let nothing be wasted.

Nahum
Long have we been careful to avoid waste. Yet the storehouses gape with emptiness. Time is a mighty eater.

Zedekiah

How long, then, thinkest thou, ere famine is upon us?

Nahum

[In low tones] Three weeks, Lord. No more.

[A pause]

Zedekiah

Three weeks ... And then?

Nahum

How can I answer thee, O King? God alone knows the answer. [Renewed silence]

Hananiah

[In great excitement] Cut the loaves in half. Cut them in three, and let that suffice for the day. Too long have they lived riotously, they and their concubines; let them grow lean, now, fighting the Lord's fight.

Abimelech

My soldiers must not have their food cut down. No man can fight on an empty stomach.

Hananiah

We must all share and share alike, the soldiers as well as the others. Jerusalem is at stake.

Abimelech

My men must have their strength kept up. Let the useless mouths go hungry, the windbags and the prattlers.

Nahum

You talk folly. What would it avail to pinch ourselves unduly, seeing that there are an hundred thousand within the walls. There is food to last us three weeks. If we slaughter the beasts reserved for the temple, we can hold out a fortnight more.

Pashur

Let us keep the peace among ourselves. Ye rail against one another like enemies. Let us stand united against Nebuchadnezzar and likewise against our own people. Neither he nor they must know aught of our need.

Zedekiah

What if he know it already?

Nahum

None can know it. Daily I set my seal on the doors of the storehouses. Neither the people nor Nebuchadnezzar can be aware of our distress.

Abimelech

God be praised. Nebuchadnezzar would show us no mercy if he knew.

Zedekiah

[After a pause] I have called you in council, elders of the people. Wars are not ended by the sword alone. I have summoned you to ask whether I should send an envoy to Nebuchadnezzar, praying him that there should be peace between our nations.

Hananiah

No peace with the blasphemers of the Almighty!

Abimelech

Let him make the first offer.

Pashur

I think it would be dangerous for us to begin. Should we open the parley, he would seek to make slaves of us.

Zedekiah

I hold other views. Though as yet he knows nothing of our desperate plight, it can remain hidden for a few days only. We must turn these days to account.

Nahum

True are thy words, O King. We must seek mercy of Nebuchadnezzar before he triumphs over us with the sword.

Abimelech

[Bitterly] Sue for mercy! Death were better!

Pashur

We need God's mercy, not man's.

Hananiah

[To Nahum] Coward and traitor!

Imre

[Wearily] When will you cease quarreling? The king's words are true. It would be folly to wait till the last hour. Let us seek parley while we can still show a bold front.

Abimelech

It is too late. The dead lying before the walls will cry reproach on us.

Pashur

It is too late. The war has heaped up such mountains of hatred.

Zedekiah

Nay, it is not too late. [He pauses for a moment] An envoy has already passed between Nebuchadnezzar and me.

[The councilors spring excitedly to their feet]

Nahum

Thou hast received an envoy from Nebuchadnezzar? Blessed be the hour.

Hananiah

Traitor! Thou holdest parley with the enemy!

Abimelech

No treaty without our consent! Thou hast forgotten.

Pashur

Thou hast held parley, King, without consulting us? Why then are we summoned in council?

Zedekiah

Peace, peace. Can ye not wait till I have finished? Ye snap at my first word like a pack of hungry hounds. [A pause. He continues more quietly] A messenger has come from Nebuchadnezzar. I have not yet heard the message. Is this to hold parley? Is this treachery? Answer!

[All are silent for a while]

Pashur

I crave thy pardon, King. It is hard to weigh one's words when so much hangs in the balance.

Zedekiah

It is for you to decide; for you to hear the envoy, or to send him away unheard.

Nahum

Our position is desperate. We must hear him.

Imre

We can listen to his message, and be cautious about accepting it.

Abimelech

We can hear him, and can settle afterwards whether we will let him return. He may be sent only to spy out the land.

Zedekiah

What say ye, Pashur and Hananiah?

Pashur

Let us hear him.

[Hananiah is silent and averts his face]

Zedekiah

Since no one opposes, we will hear the message. [Going to the doorway he calls out] Joab, fetch the envoy. [Zedekiah returns to the table] Let each ask what questions he will. But our answers must show one mind.

[Baruch is ushered in by Joab. The latter passes out again, replacing the curtain. Baruch bows before the king]

Dost thou bring a message to Israel from King Nebuchadnezzar?

Baruch

He has sent me with a message to thee, O King.

Zedekiah

These are my councilors. Who speaks to me speaks to them also, for they and I, Israel and Israel's king, are at one by God's will. [Turning to the others] Question him.

Hananiah

[Scornfully] What grace does the king of the heathen vouchsafe ...

Abimelech

[Interrupting] Let us consider practical matters first! What is your name?

Baruch

Baruch, son of Zebulon, of the house of Naphtali.

Abimelech

Are you then of our blood?

Baruch

I am a servant of the one God, and was born in Jerusalem.

Abimelech

Does anyone here know this man?

Pashur

I know his father, a just man, and a faithful servant of the Lord.

Abimelech

How did you fall into the enemy's hands?

Baruch

I was drawing water from Moria well when they seized me.

Abimelech

What proof have you that you are an envoy? Have you a letter, signed and sealed?

Baruch

Nebuchadnezzar gave me his signet ring, that I might pass the sentries going and returning. [He shows the ring on his finger.]

Abimelech

I have no more questions to ask. Let him deliver his message.

Baruch

When the Assyrian soldiers waylaid me, they took me to the king's tent. Nebuchadnezzar has kept me under guard these eleven months. Sending for me yesterday, he said: "Wilt thou take my message to King Zedekiah?" Standing before him without fear, I answered: "I will." Then spake Nebuchadnezzar: "Eleven months have I laid siege to this town. I have sworn that not again will I lie with woman until the gates of Jerusalem have been opened. But I will wait no longer. Should King Zedekiah wish for terms, let him hasten. Never has an enemy withstood me more stoutly. To none will I be more gentle than to him, should he hasten to sue for mercy."

Abimelech

Nebuchadnezzar is a great warrior. It is an honor to have held out against him for eleven months.

Baruch

He said further: "If ye open the gates and humble yourselves ere the moon be full, I will grant you your lives. Every man may dwell in safety under his vine and under his fig tree. Though ye have shed our blood, I seek not yours, but only victory and renown. It is my will that from sunrise to sunset the nations should learn the news that none can withstand my sword; that there is no king but shall bow before me, the king of kings. I need but a sign, and your city shall be safe, your days long in the land."

Nahum

Methinks the terms are easy.

Pashur

Too easy for me to trust them.

Zedekiah

But the sign! What sign does Nebuchadnezzar demand?

Baruch

He said: "Zedekiah, who has taken up arms against me, must abase himself. When I enter the city, let him walk to meet me, from the gates of the temple to the wall, carrying his crown in his hands, and wearing a wooden yoke on his neck ..."

Zedekiah

[Drawing himself up] A yoke?

Baruch

"A yoke that all men may know his stubbornness is broken and his pride humbled. I will meet him, will lift the yoke from his neck, and replace the crown on his head."

Zedekiah

Never shall the man wear a crown whose neck has borne a yoke. Never! [He rises to his feet]

Abimelech

I could not endure it! [He also rises]

[The others remain seated and silent. After a long pause, Nahum speaks meditatively]

Nahum

From the gates of the temple to the wall?

Pashur

It is barely an hundred paces.

Imre

No more than seventy, I think. No more than seventy.

Zedekiah

[Turning fiercely upon them] Ye reckon up the paces I am to take, with my neck yoked like an ox drawing the plough? Are ye all mad to think that I shall so humble myself? Did ye show courage only while your own lives were at stake? Do ye think nothing of my shame, if ye can make your own peace? Cowards all!

Pashur

Thou hast sworn, O King, that each of us should speak freely the words which came to his mouth.

Zedekiah

Thou dost well to remind me. Pardon my anger. Speak freely.

Nahum

I beseech thee to accept the terms, not for our sake alone but for that of our children.

For the sake of our country.

For temple and altar.

For God, who commands it.

[Abimelech is silent, hiding his face]

[Paces up and down, as the struggle rages within him. At length he steps up to the table, and speaks in solemn tones] I will do what ye demand, breaking my pride like a potter's vessel, bowing my neck beneath the yoke.

[All move to speak, but he imposes silence, and continues]

I will take the crown from my head, and offer it up with my hands, as is enjoined. But holy is the crown of Israel, and none shall wear it whose neck hath borne a yoke. When I have put off from me the wood of shame, I shall put away likewise sceptre and ring, consigning both to my son. Young is he, but ye will counsel him. Swear that ye will be true to him, so that the people may look up to him. Swear that ye will invest him with crown and with ring.

[Greatly moved] I swear it, O King.

We swear it.

As a king hast thou acted. Praised be thy name.

Nahum

Eternal honor to King Zedekiah.

Zedekiah

Thus shall the walls stand fast, thus shall the holy city be saved, though I sink into the dust. Better I should perish than Zion. Jerusalem endureth for ever.

All

[Fervently] Jerusalem endureth for ever.

Zedekiah

[To Baruch] Thou hearest, boy? Go, then, to the king of Ashur, and say unto him: "Zedekiah, who hath been ruler, and hath taken up arms against thee, boweth himself before thee, that thou mayest show him thy mercy." Hasten, that soon I may stand before the door of my house, saying to my people the precious word, "Peace".

Baruch

[Disquieted, speaks in subdued tones] I hear, Lord King. But there is yet one other thing I have to tell thee, one more demand from the king of Ashur.

Abimelech

[Angrily] Yet more? Does not this shame suffice him?

Baruch

A trifle he termed it. It looms large in my mind.

Zedekiah

What does his pride still crave?

Baruch

He spake unto me and said: "I will take the yoke from the king's neck and restore the crown to his head. He shall walk at my left hand, that men may know I honor him as my royal brother. But there is still one within your walls, of whom folk say that he is mightier than any. I would see this mighty one. They say that there is a god within your walls, whose countenance ye hide behind the curtains of a tabernacle, for that no one can bear to look upon him. To me, fear is unknown, and I wish to enter his presence, that I may behold him. I will not lay hands on his altar, nor touch his bread, neither will I covet his treasures. One thing only do I ask, that I may enter his tabernacle, for I would fain set eyes on him who hath proved mightier than I." Thus spake Nebuchadnezzar.

Pashur

Never! Never!

Hananiah

The fire of the Lord consume him for the sacrilegious thought.

Pashur

Better that the temple should crumble to dust, than that the tabernacle should be desecrated.

Imre

[In consternation] He would look upon the holy of holies! Terrible is the request.

Pashur

Unbounded is the insolence of the heathen ruler! Dismiss his messenger, Lord King. Send back the envoy.

Hananiah

Send back the envoy. Never must such a thing be.

Nahum

Be not too hasty, O King. In our hands lies the welfare of the nation.

Abimelech

A thousand deaths were better than this shame.

Pashur

I will face death with you, will perish in the midst of your warriors.

Hananiah

[Savagely] Dismiss the envoy. Rather death than this sacrilege.

Imre

Ye talk lightly of dying. Bethink ye that your pride means seventy thousand deaths.

Pashur

Would you profane God's holy of holies?

Imre

Life is part of God's holiness. God himself is life.

Hananiah

It would be an everlasting disgrace could the heathen look on the face of Jehovah.

Nahum

Let our foes exult; let our pride be humbled. So be it, if the city outlast our pride and our lives. King Zedekiah, save Jerusalem!

Hananiah

Nay, dismiss the envoy.

Zedekiah

I am naught but the hand holding the scales. I stand aloof from your decision. Make up your minds. Count your votes. Speed ye, that the matter may be settled for good or for ill.

Imre

I am the oldest among you. My word is, let us comply with Nebuchadnezzar's demands.

Hananiah

Let us refuse. God will help us. Let us refuse.

Pashur

I will not chaffer with God's majesty. Never will I consent to such impiety.

Nahum

Let God's city stand for ever. Accept the terms.

Zedekiah

What sayest thou, Abimelech?

Abimelech

Not for me to advise thee, King Zedekiah. Not for me, who am but thy servant and thy sword. By yes and by no, in life and in death, do I stand by thy decision.

Zedekiah

Two votes against two, and in my own mind there are voices twain! Conflict without; conflict within. I hold aloof, leaving it to you to direct my will. You cast it back to me like seadrift, and, trembling, I am still constrained to decide. Have I, indeed, to throw these dreadful dice?

Pashur

God will give thee light.

Zedekiah

Ah, would he but speak to me. Happy our forefathers to whom he appeared in a cloud. I stretch forth my hands towards him, but still for me the voice of heaven is dumb. I grope in the darkness, finding I know not what. Pray for me that I may be rightly guided.

Nahum

Thou hast our love, O King.

Zedekiah

Time presses. Ere the night is spent I must say yes or no; where perchance no is yes, and yes is no. God give me light. [He rises to his feet and all rise with him] Leave me to myself. The cleavage among you increases my own indecision. I shall act as my heart dictates, and it may well be that ere ye reach home I shall have made my choice, for my soul travaileth. Pray, friends, pray, that my choice may be the best for Israel. Pray for me, pray for Jerusalem.

Pashur
God give thee light. I shall not close my eyes in sleep until thou hast chosen. I will hold vigil before the altar.

Hananiah
Remember God.

Nahum
Remember the city.

Imre
Remember the children, remember the women.

Abimelech
I abide by thy choice in life or in death.

[All depart, leaving Baruch and the king]

Baruch
[Quietly] Shall I, too, take my leave, King Zedekiah?

Zedekiah
[Collecting his thoughts] What sayest thou? Nay, thou must remain.

[Baruch stands by the doorway while Zedekiah walks restlessly to and fro for a time. Then, pausing by the window, the king stares over the town, subsequently resuming his restless pacing. At length he turns and speaks to Baruch]

Zedekiah
Nebuchadnezzar demands an answer to-day?

Baruch

Yea, Lord; for to-morrow the moon is full.

Zedekiah

[Paces the floor again. Then abruptly] Thou sawest him face to face. Did he ask thee anything concerning me?

Baruch

His chief counselor and his scribe were present. The former asked me about you, but Nebuchadnezzar bade him be silent.

Zedekiah

Full of pride is he, and his wrath is like a storm over our heads. But I fear him not. Himself, he asked nothing concerning me?

Baruch

Nothing, Lord King.

Zedekiah

To him we are naught. To him our walls are but a handful of dust. Yet we can meet defiance with defiance. For eleven months he has been breaking his teeth against the ramparts of the city, and he would dismiss us with a smile. I am not worth a word, and he rates our town at a breath. Nevertheless my yoke is not yet ready; the walls of Jerusalem still stand. We have taught him to wait, but he has not yet learned his lesson. Shall I be the slave of his caprices? He would tarry but a day? Let him tarry for weeks and months. [Drawing himself up] Take this message to Nebuchadnezzar. Say unto him ...

Baruch

[In alarm] Decide not in anger, King Zedekiah.

Zedekiah

[Rigid with astonishment] How darest thou interrupt me?

Baruch

[Kneels] I implore thee, save Jerusalem. Stretch forth thine hand in peace, lest the walls crumble and the temple be shattered. Lord King, I adjure thee, open the gates, open thy heart.

Zedekiah

[Wrathfully] "Open the gates, open thy heart". I have heard those words before. They have been put into thy mouth. One stands behind thee speaking against me with thy voice.

Baruch

Nay, Lord King. My supplication arises from the depths of my heart. Something will I tell thee, which hitherto I have withheld. It was not at Nebuchadnezzar's summons that I went to him, but of my own free will, hoping that I might soften his heart. I saw that either side waited for the other to propose peace. Day after day, for eleven long months, did I importune him till he sent me with this message.

Zedekiah

Thou, a boy, a child? While we were holding counsel, thou soughtest out the king of kings to seek peace and ensure it?

Baruch

This did I, O King, in the urgency of my heart's wishes.

Zedekiah

[Regards him fixedly for a time. Then, speaking sharply] Not thine own deed, this, nor thy thought.

Baruch

I went at no man's orders.

Zedekiah

Thou speakest falsely. No boy could conceive such a deed for himself.

Baruch

I swear to thee that I did it unadvised. He knew naught of it, neither commanded it nor approved.

Zedekiah

He? Who is he of whose orders thou speakest?

Baruch

[Evasively] My teacher, my master.

Zedekiah

Who is thy master, who? I would know who issues commands to the boys of this city.

Baruch

God's servant and prophet is my master. Men call him Jeremiah.

Zedekiah

[Furiously] Jeremiah, always Jeremiah. Ever the shadow that follows my deeds, ever in revolt against me. I have cast him into a dungeon, but still, as in the beginning, rises his clamor for peace. Why this persecution? Why?

Baruch

Thou art mistaken. Jeremiah hath more love for thee than for any other in this town.

Zedekiah

I need not his love. I spew forth his love, and I despise his anger. Who is he, that he should dare to love me? Shall one venture to stand up in the streets and give tongue, declaring that he loveth me, or loveth me not? Why should Jeremiah push in twixt me and my resolve? Would he show himself the greater of us twain? I am the king, I alone! Let him cry, Peace, peace! Not in his hand lieth the fate of Jerusalem. I am king in Zion, and never shall he boast that he frightened me with his dreams. Better the city should perish, than be saved by the hand of Jeremiah. Go thou to Nebuchadnezzar and say unto him: Never will Zedekiah bear a yoke. Never shall the king of Ashur raise the curtain before the holy of holies.

Nebuchadnezzar may come with all his men; he will find Zedekiah ready to meet him.

[Baruch raising both hands imploringly, is about to speak. Zedekiah continues]

Not a word. If thou failest to carry my message, I will have Jeremiah's head.

[Again Baruch endeavors to speak]

A single word, and Jeremiah's life is forfeit. Away, I command thee, away!

[Baruch stands for a moment, and then, veiling his face, passes out. Zedekiah draws himself up threateningly when Baruch hesitates. As soon as the young man has gone, the king lowers his outstretched arm, and his countenance is once more shadowed with anxiety. Then he draws a deep breath and speaks]

Zedekiah
It is finished. No longer the torture of indecision.

[He paces to and fro once more. Then he stamps twice. Joab enters]

Joab
The king calls?

Zedekiah
Wine, bring me wine. I need sleep, deep and dreamless sleep.

[Joab brings a pitcher and fills a silver goblet. Zedekiah empties it at a draught. Then he listens, and his face is again clouded]

Who is walking outside there? I hear footsteps. Does the spy still tarry?

Joab

He has gone forth, Lord. You hear the sentry, my brother Nehemiah.

Zedekiah

Tell him to tread softly when he is on guard outside my bedchamber at night. I need sleep just as much as other men.

Joab

I will see to it, Lord. [He draws aside the curtains of the bed and veils the lamp. Now the only light in the room comes from the pale moonbeams] Shall I read from the scriptures, Lord King, as heretofore?

Zedekiah

Nay, not even the scriptures can help me. I would fain sleep, even as other men sleep. My lids ache and my heart aches likewise.

[Joab helps him to remove his outer garment. Zedekiah flings himself on the couch]

Joab

God guard thy slumbers, O King.

[Joab calls Nehemiah. Silently the two stand at the head of the bed, motionless figures holding spears. In the moonlight their shadows rise in giant silhouettes on the wall. The only sound is the gentle plashing of a fountain in the court-yard]

Zedekiah

[Springing up with a wild cry] Why do ye whisper together? Did I not command ye to silence?

Joab

[Alarmed] We said nothing, Lord King.

Zedekiah

Some one is talking. Who is it that devours my slumber? All should sleep, so that I too may sleep. Is there anyone awake in the neighboring rooms?

Joab

No one, Lord King. Nor anywhere throughout the palace.

Zedekiah

So I alone hold vigil. Why should all the burden be laid upon me? All the walls of the city, all the towers of care? Get me wine.

[Joab fills the goblet once more. Zedekiah drains it and flings it away. With a groan he lies down again. All is still save for the murmur of the fountain. Zedekiah, who has been lying motionless on the bed, now very quietly sits up in the gloom. Crouching like a wild beast about to spring, he listens intently. Then he suddenly screams]

Zedekiah

Some one is speaking. I hear a voice which drones unendingly. I have given orders that none shall speak in my house. The voice is chanting. But I have forbidden that any should sing under my roof. Do ye not hear it?

Joab

I hear nothing, Lord.

Nehemiah

No sound has reached me.

Zedekiah

[Glares at the two lads. Crouching he listens for a moment, and breaks forth again] I hear it, I tell you; an interminable monotone. Listen, Joab, here where I am listening. It is somewhere beneath us, burrowing like a mole in the darkness of my slumber, devouring my sleep. Canst not hear, lad?

Joab

[Listens intently for a moment, and then shudders] I hear a voice rising from the depths. Like the voice of one singing. The spirits of the deep are awake beneath the house. The voice laments and moans like a caged beast.

Nehemiah
Perchance it is but the wind moaning through a cranny.

Zedekiah
I hear words; I feel them without understanding them. Who dares to sing by night in my house? Is it so well with my slaves that they must sing while I toss sleepless? Away, Joab, and silence the disturber.

[Joab hastens out. Zedekiah crouches, listening. He seems at first to hear something. Then he raises his head, and subsequently lowers it to listen once more. Suddenly three dull blows are heard. The king listens eagerly. He draws a breath of relief]

God be praised, the voice is stilled.

[Joab reenters with troubled mien]

Who was talking?

Joab
[Trembling] I know not, Lord, I did not find him. As I neared the marketplace, the noise of singing came to me louder, rising as it were from the depths of the earth. I followed the direction of the sound. There was no one singing in the marketplace. The utterance had a hollow ring, as if it came from a well or from a pit. Now I could hear the words, and they were terrible. Thrice did I strike the ground with the haft of my spear. Then was the Gehenna silent.

Zedekiah
What were the words?

Joab
[Shuddering] I dare not repeat them.

Zedekiah
Tell me the words, I command thee.

Joab
It was blasphemy that rose from the pit.

Zedekiah
Repeat the words, if you fear my anger.

Joab
[Complies. His voice rises in a psalm]
I have forsaken mine house,
I have cast off mine heritage;
I have given the dearly beloved of my soul
Into the hand of her enemies.
My tears run down like a river day and night,
For grievous is the affliction
Of the daughter of my people.

Zedekiah
[With a loud cry] Jeremiah! Always Jeremiah.

Joab

[Continuing to chant as if inspired]
He hath given up into the hand of the enemy
The walls of her palaces;
They have made a noise in the house of the Lord,
As in the day of a solemn feast.
He hath ...

Zedekiah
Be still, be still. I will hear no more. Always Jeremiah, and again Jeremiah.
Wherever I go he stands at the cross roads; his challenge rings behind all
my doings; he forces his way into my dreams, and feeds my indecision.

How can I outrun this terrible shadow? He cries to me even from the pit.
Who will free me from him?

Joab

Lord, if he be thine enemy, say the word ... [He makes a movement with
his spear]

Zedekiah

[Startled out of his anger, looks at the lad wonderingly. Then, with
awakening pride] Thou wouldst ... Nay, I fear him not. I fear no man. Nor
am I certain if he be my enemy. I was foolish, perhaps, to flee from him.
Who can tell? [He paces the room] Joab!

Joab

My Lord?

Zedekiah

Go forth, taking with thee thy brother Nehemiah. Open the pit and bring
hither the man ye will find there. None must know that he enters and
leaves the palace.

[Joab and Nehemiah pass out. The king soliloquizes in low tones]

At every cross road, behind my back, always too late and always
compelling me to listen. Why did I appeal only to God, who vouchsafes
me no answer? Why did I not hearken to those who say that he declares
his will through their mouths? But wherefore do they speak with
conflicting voices? How could I discern the false from the true? Dread is
this God who will not break silence, and whose messengers cannot be
certainly known.

[Jeremiah enters accompanied by the two lads. At a sign from Zedekiah,
Joab unveils the lamp. Then he and Nehemiah withdraw. Jeremiah is pale
and emaciated. His dark eyes flash from a white and bony face, looking
almost as if set in a skull. He regards the king with a questioning calm.
After a momentary embarrassment the king speaks]

Zedekiah

I sent for thee, Jeremiah, to ask why thou dost disturb my rest. Why singest thou in the night when others sleep?

Jeremiah

He may not sleep who watches over the people. The Lord hath appointed me to watch and to give warning.

Zedekiah

Jeremiah, I have summoned thee to hold counsel with me. No man knoweth that to this end I have drawn thee from the pit where thou hast been prisoned. Wilt thou advise me truly?

Jeremiah

God helping me, I will.

Zedekiah

Know, then, what none other knows save my innermost counselors. An envoy has come from Nebuchadnezzar, seeking to end the war between our nations.

Jeremiah

[Exultantly] God be praised! Open the gates, open thy heart to humbleness.

Zedekiah

Rejoice not too soon. Hard are the terms and measureless is the arrogancy of the king of Ashur.

Jeremiah

Arrogant hast thou been towards him, therefore must thou accept arrogancy in return. Put compulsion on thy heart, so thou save Jerusalem from destruction.

Zedekiah

He asks my honor.

Jeremiah

Sacrifice thine honor for the city.

Zedekiah

Is not honor my office; is not pride my crown?

Jeremiah

If they be truly thine, cast them from thee. Peace is better than honor; suffering is better than death.

Zedekiah

He would bow my neck beneath a yoke.

Jeremiah

Blessed is he who suffers for all; who suffers that all may live. Bow thy neck, and save the city.

Zedekiah

I should bring shame on all the kings whose throne is my heritage; I should disgrace the mantle of my forefathers.

Jeremiah

Think no longer of those who have been. They are dead, and worms have eaten them. Think of the city and of those who now live therein.

Zedekiah

Not me alone will Nebuchadnezzar abase, but God also.

Jeremiah

God smiles at those who would abase him. Open the gates, open thy heart to humbleness.

Zedekiah

Nebuchadnezzar would enter the holy of holies which none may approach.

Jeremiah

God will avert it, should it be his will; thou canst not avert it. Open the gates, open thy heart to humbleness.

Zedekiah

[Angrily] Thy wisdom is stubbornness; thy counsel, insolence. With deaf ears dost thou hearken, and thine answer is hard as flint.

Jeremiah

Am I to laud thy blindness, to approve whate'er thou sayest? Feigning to ask counsel, thou wouldst have naught but flattery. May my tongue consume away in my mouth, my bones fall apart, ere I praise thy folly and cease from crying against thy blindness.

Zedekiah

Why railest thou thus, when thou hast not yet heard my purpose?

Jeremiah

I know thy purpose. With words dost thou fawn on me, whilst thy will is set up against me. Wouldst mock me, and play with God's word? Thou hast not summoned me to help thee decide. Long ere this has the message been signed and sealed within thy soul. Thou mayst deceive thyself, King of Israel, but me thou canst not deceive.

Zedekiah

Jeremiah!

Jeremiah

Yea, verily, I, Jeremiah, say unto thee, the king: Thou dealest falsely with me, and thy words are a blind. No longer is thy will free, nor dost thou truly desire me to influence thy decision.

Zedekiah

[Unsteadily] How canst thou know this?

Jeremiah

Thy lips betray thee. Thou quailest before my wrath like a guilty man. Fain wouldst thou tempt me to approve thy decision, to lift the guilt from thy shoulders. Woe unto him who tempts men, for he tempts the god that is in men.

Zedekiah

[Hesitates, greatly moved. Then he speaks in low tones] Much, indeed, is it given thee to know, Jeremiah. Too true are thy words. My will is no longer free, I have delivered my message to the envoy.

Jeremiah

Recall it! Save the city.

Zedekiah

He is on his way to Nebuchadnezzar.

Jeremiah

Send for him! Bring him back!

Zedekiah

Too late. The advice comes too late.

Jeremiah

Hasten after him. Pursue him with runners and riders.

Zedekiah

It is too late. By now my message must have reached the king of Ashur.

Jeremiah

[Hides his face, lamenting] Woe, woe unto Jerusalem, woe unto Jerusalem!

Zedekiah

[Drawing near him in alarm] What ails thee Jeremiah?

154

[Jeremiah does not heed the king. Sobs shake his frame. Soon, however, he draws himself up once more. Now his gaze is fixed on the distance. He speaks as in a dream, raising his hands, like one inspired]

Jeremiah
How art thou fallen from heaven,
Jerusalem, sun of the morning!
Thou hast said in thine heart,
I will ascend into heaven,
I will ascend above the heights of the clouds.
Alas, thou art fallen from glory,
Art sunken in darkness and night.

Zedekiah
[Calls to him loudly, hoping to awaken him from the trance] Jeremiah!

Jeremiah
What star was brighter than thine,
Thou city of Jacob,
Thou fortress of David,
Thou tabernacle of Solomon,
God's treasure and his holy house?
Who could herald thy ways, who could signal thy praise?
All happy the psalteries, the cymbals grew light,
With sounding thy triumphs from morning till night.

Zedekiah
Thou ravest, Jeremiah; awake, awake!

Jeremiah
[Unheeding]
How still art thou now, my beloved.
Thy brightness, say, where hath it gone?
The voice of the bridegroom and the voice of the bride
No longer are heard among thy houses.
The market hath become desolate.
Quenched are the voice of joy,

The voice of gladness,
The sound of flute playing,
And the song of the maidens.
A slayer hath fallen upon thee,
An avenger from the north.
Waste places are thy streets,
Nettles grow in thy pleasant places,
Thorns and brambles in the palace of thy kings.
Alas, thy walls are laid low,
All thy towers are broken down;
Shamefully overthrown
Is the everlasting heart of thy sanctuary.

Zedekiah
Accursèd one, thou liest! High and hale stand the walls of Jerusalem.

Jeremiah
[With growing frenzy]
Every head hath been shorn,
Every beard hath been clipt.
The mothers, wearing sackcloth,
Tear the flesh from their cheeks,
Wailing:
"Where are my sons, where are my daughters?"
Woe is me!
The dead bodies of the sons
Lie like dung in the streets
Where they have perished by the sword;
The daughters have been strangled with their own hair,
And the women with child have been ripped up.
The jackals of the wilderness are gorged,
The ravens weary with feasting.

Zedekiah
Be silent, be silent! Thou liest!

Jeremiah
What availeth it to seek safety in thorny thickets,
To flee from death into the burning fissures of the rock?
They hunt thee with horses, with companies of spearmen,
Track thee down, and with sticks beat the coverts for their game,
Drive thee forth from the crannies with firebrands and smoke,
Pursue thee, and seize thee, and slay.
They ravish the women, they slaughter the elders,
Just men are made slaves of their lowliest bondsmen,
Made servants of servants the daughters of kings.

Zedekiah
Hold thy peace, liar, lest my wrath smite thee!

Jeremiah
[Lamenting]
Jerusalem, virgin and daughter of Judah,
The heathen make mock of thy pitiful plight.
Woe is me that I must look on thine affliction.
All thine enemies have opened their mouths against thee,
Laughing, and hissing, and gnashing their teeth,
Saying:
"We have swallowed her up!
"Is this the city that men call
"The perfection of beauty,
"The joy of the whole earth?
"Verily we have laid her low.
"Certainly this is the day we looked for,
"We have found it,
"We have seen it."

Zedekiah
[Beside himself with rage, clenching his fists] Be silent, liar, I will listen
no longer.

Jeremiah
Jerusalem, holy city of the Lord,

Cradle of the nations, treasure of the world!
Who will extol thee, who now will search thee out?
A legend of the ages hast thou become,
A fable and a proverb among the peoples.
Ah, I see ...

Zedekiah

Raving madman, naught more shalt thou see.

Jeremiah

I see thy suffering, I witness thy death,
I see ...

Zedekiah

[Grappling with him, bursts out in a fury] Naught more shalt thou see! I will have thee blinded.

Jeremiah

[Stares around, as if suddenly and dreadfully awakened. Then laughing loudly, he chants with renewed frenzy]
Me?
Blind me? Nay, ruthless one,
Not such is the purpose of God.
Know well that one shall be blinded
Ere these days draw to a close.
'Tis one with eyes that see not,
With ears that will not hear.
Yet hearken now, King Zedekiah!

[Zedekiah releases Jeremiah, and regards him with amazement and terror. Jeremiah raises his hands in denunciation, and continues]

Thee
Shall they seize,
The servants of Ashur,
Seize thee in God's temple which thou hast destroyed.

158

They tear thee away from the horns of the altar,
To which thy hands cleave in the vain hope of help.
Naught availeth thy sword, for they break it in sunder,
Then bind thine arms straitly with fetters of brass,
Haling thee forth and the stairway adown;
Like a beast for the sacrifice scourging thee on;
To him will they bring thee whose hand thou rejectedst;
To him will they bring thee whose yoke thou hast broken,
To him who thy fiery doom will have spoken.

[Zedekiah has retreated several steps, and makes gestures as if to avert the threatened fate]

To thy knees as they force thee with curses and blows,
In the air-blast the furnace roars fiercely and glows.
Now the iron is heated, gleaming red, flashing white.
In thine eyeballs they plunge it, the scorching steel.
Thy flesh smokes and hisses, thy senses reel.
God's daylight has vanished in infinite night.

[Zedekiah screams, and claps his hands to his eyes as if blinded]

But ere thy sight, in a fiery mist
Of blood and tears, is forever gone,
Thy sons, by the sharp sword fiercely kissed,
Shall be slain in thy presence, one by one,
As the headsman's blade flashes through flesh and through bone.
Bootless thy struggles; the slaves hold thee fast!
The first falls, the second, the third and last!
They are sped, and thy weeping and wailing are vain.
Their blood drenches the ground, while thou, in thy pain,
Ere the burning steel seareth the sight from thine eyes,
Seest how Israel's race and kingship dies.

Zedekiah

[Groping his way across the room like a blind man, staggers to the couch. Now he puts up his hands beseechingly] Mercy! Have mercy!

Jeremiah

By thy cries all in vain will the darkness be riven,
As thou liftest thy hands to the unseen heaven,
God's mercy imploring! God no mercy will show
To the king whose false pride Zion's temple laid low.
He casteth thee down among worms which are blind,
Which crawl on their bellies, each after his kind.
With despised and rejected, the sick, the forsworn,
Shalt thou walk, Zedekiah, debased and forlorn,
Consorting with lepers, with halt and with lame,
Among outcasts the poorest. Thus thy pride God shall tame.
With beggars shall harbor; a beggar thyself,
Wearing sackcloth and ashes, shalt pass through the land.
Those who know thee—once splendent in power and in pelf,
King erstwhile in Zion—uplifting the hand,
Shall curse thee, Zedekiah.

Zedekiah

[Utterly crushed by the adjuration, has collapsed, groaning, on to the couch. Now he slowly rises, and contemplates Jeremiah blankly] What a power is entrusted to thee, Jeremiah. Thou hast broken the strength of my limbs. The very marrow is frozen in my bones. Terrible are thy words, Jeremiah.

Jeremiah

[He has awakened from his trance, and the fire in his eyes is quenched] Poor are my words, Zedekiah. Weakness is all my strength. I know, but cannot act!

Zedekiah

Why didst thou not come to me sooner?

Jeremiah

I was ever at hand, but thou couldst not find me.

Zedekiah

Thou hast filled my heart with dread, yet I bear thee no grudge. There must be no quarrel betwixt us twain who stand in the shadow of death. Get thee back whence thou hast come. Thou shalt not lack food, for I will share my last crust with thee. Let none know of our converse, save God. [Jeremiah turns to go] Stay, Jeremiah. Must the fate be, which thou hast foretold? Jerusalem, my Jerusalem. Canst thou not avert it?

Jeremiah

[Gloomily] Naught can I do to avert it. I can only prophesy. Woe upon the impotent.

Zedekiah

[After a pause] Jeremiah, I did not want war. I was forced to declare war, but I loved peace. And I love thee because of thy love for peace. Not with a light heart did I take up arms, but before I lived there was war under God's heaven, and there will be war after I am dead. I have suffered greatly, as thou canst testify when the time comes. Be thou near me when thy words are fulfilled.

Jeremiah

I will be near thee, Zedekiah, my brother. [Slowly he averts his face from the king and moves towards the doorway]

Zedekiah

Jeremiah! [Jeremiah turns] Thou hast cursed me, Jeremiah. Bless me now, ere we part.

Jeremiah

[After a moment's hesitation, strides back and holds his hands over the king] The Lord bless thee, and keep thee in all thy ways. May the light of his countenance shine upon thee, and may he give thee peace.

Zedekiah

[As in a dream] May he give us peace.

THE SUPREME AFFLICTION

SCENE SEVEN

I gave my back to the smiters, and my cheeks to them that pluck off the hair: I hid not my face from shame and spitting. Isaiah L, 6.

SCENE SEVEN

The following morning; the great square before the temple. A large crowd, consisting chiefly of women and children, is swarming up the steps leading to the palace, shouting and screaming. The leaders of the mob have reached the palace door, and are hammering on it with their fists.

The Doorkeeper
[Appearing through a wicket which he closes behind him] Are you still there? I have told you already that no more bread will be given out to-day.

A Woman
But I am hungry.

A Second Woman
You gave me one tiny loaf for my three children, a loaf no larger than my fist. Look at my little girl here; see how skinny her fingers are. [She lifts the child to show him]

A Third Woman
Look at mine too. [She also shows her child]

Confused and Angry Voices
I am hungry.—Give me bread.—We are hungry.—Bread.—Bread.

Another Voice
Let us have the keys.

Voices
Yes.—Give us the keys.—Open the storehouses.

The Doorkeeper
[Pushing back the foremost among the mob] Away with you! The king's orders are that everyone shall have a loaf at daybreak. Then the storehouses are to be closed.

A Voice

I got no loaf.

Other Voices

Nor I, nor I.

A Woman

You could hardly see mine; and I have a child at the breast. Justice!

A Second

Mine was full of sand and gravel.

A Third

They are not the same loaves we used to get. We are being cheated. Justice!

The Doorkeeper

Nahum treats you all alike. He is perfectly fair.

A Voice

Where is he?

Other Voices

Where is he? We want to see him.—Let him show himself.—We will talk to him.—He is a thief.—Where is he?

Another Voice

[Shouting stridently] He sits at home and fattens up his own household. They bake cake for themselves.

A Second Voice

Yes, the rich have hoarded all they need.

Voices

While we go hungry.—Bread for the poor.—Bread, bread.

The Strident Voice

The king has golden dishes filled with dainties. In the palace they would rather throw their leavings to the dogs than feed our children.

A Voice

I don't believe that.

Other Voices

Yes.—Yes.—I have seen them do it.—My sister says they do.—Where is Nahum?—Give us bread.

[Gradually the voices fuse into a single shout for bread. The mob thronging the steps grows more threatening. Some of those in the front ranks are about to seize the doorkeeper, while others continue to beat on the closed door. The doorkeeper blows a trumpet]

Abimelech

[Hastening from the palace, attended by a number of soldiers] Away with you. Push them back. Down the steps. Clear the entrance to the palace.

[The soldiers use the hafts of their spears freely, and the mob yields ground, panicstricken]

Voices

He struck me.—They are killing us.—Where is my child?—Help.—Help!

[The crowd forms again at the foot of the steps, and faces Abimelech angrily]

Abimelech

Are you all mad? The enemy is attacking us. Since dawn I have been on the ramparts to marshal the defence, and you meanwhile are raising a tumult at our backs. What would ye, rabble?

Voices

Bread.—We are hungry.—Bread.—Our children have nothing to eat.

Abimelech

Everyone has had his loaf.

Voices

Not I.—They left me out.—Not enough.

Abimelech

The town is besieged. You must make the most of what you have. We are at war.

Voices

There is not enough bread.—We are hungry.

Abimelech

Well, be hungry! We are shedding our blood for you. The city must be our first care. [Trying to hearten them up he exclaims] Jerusalem for ever!

A Voice

[Half-heartedly] Jerusalem for ever!

The Strident Voice

Who or what is Jerusalem? Has Jerusalem a stomach? Has Jerusalem blood? The stones and the walls are not Jerusalem. We are Jerusalem.

Voices

Yes, we are Jerusalem.—Give us life.—Give us food.—Feed our children.— What is Jerusalem to me? I want bread.

Abimelech

[Stamping fiercely] Be silent, all. Back to your homes. Why do you loiter in the marketplace? Do you not know that we are at war?

A Woman

Why are we at war?

Voices

Yes, why?—Why are we at war?—Let us make peace.—Peace.—Peace.—
Bread.

The Strident Voice

Was it not well with us under Nebuchadnezzar? Was not his yoke light?
Were not our days pleasant?

Voices

Yea, yea.—Peace with Nebuchadnezzar.—End the war.—Down with the
war.—A curse on him who began the war.

A Woman

It was Zedekiah's doing. He wanted war to help his friends the Egyptians.

Voices

Yes, he has betrayed us.—While we suffer, he lies at ease among his wives.

Abimelech

Who dares to slander the Lord's anointed. He is ever in the forefront of
the battle.

The Strident Voice

It is false.

Abimelech

Who says it is false? Let him stand forth and face my sword. Who says it?
[The crowd is silent] Beware of slanderers! Now then, off home with you.
Let those who can fight, man the walls.

Voices

[From the back] Nahum, Nahum! Here he comes. [The crowd surges
round Nahum] Nahum, good Nahum.—Give us bread.—Bread.—Bread.—
You will treat us fairly.—Help us.—Good Nahum.

Nahum

[Elbowing his way through the press] Let me pass!

The Crowd

[Follows him up the steps] Nahum! Nahum!

Abimelech

Back! Stand back.

[The soldiers raise their spears, and the crowd shrinks away to the foot of the steps]

Nahum

What would ye?

A Voice

Open the storehouses.

Nahum

The storehouses are empty. Each of you has a loaf every day. That must suffice.

Voices

I have had no loaf.—Nor I.—Open the storehouses.

Nahum

I tell you they are empty.

The Strident Voice

Let us see for ourselves.

Voices

Yes, let us see for ourselves.—I don't believe it.—Open the storehouses.—Let us see for ourselves.

Nahum

I swear to you ...

The Strident Voice

When we see we will believe. We have been cheated too long.

Voices

They are all cheats, the priests, the king, all.—Give up the keys.—How they lied when they prophesied victory. [The voices become more menacing] Where are the Egyptians?—Zedekiah promised that the Egyptians would help us.—Where are the signs and wonders?—Bread, bread, bread.—Give up the keys.

[The mob surges up the steps once more, surrounding Nahum and endeavoring to snatch the keys]

Nahum

Help, help!

Abimelech

[Beating them back, aided by his men] Down, down!

A Voice

Oh, I am wounded. See, I bleed!

Abimelech

For the last time. To your homes! Clear the marketplace, or I shall use my sword.

The Strident Voice

The marketplace and the city belong to us.

[A messenger appears at the back of the crowd]

Messenger

Abimelech! Where is Abimelech?

Abimelech

Here.

The Crowd

There he is, the wretch, the murderer!

Messenger

Help, Abimelech. They have broken in at Moria Gate.

[Cries of terror arise from the crowd]

Abimelech

[Cutting a path through them with his sword] Make way, make way.

[He strides off. Doorkeeper, Nahum, and the soldiers withdraw through the wicket]

[The crowd becomes chaotic. Previously it had been animated by a definite will. Now its units form a confused medley of horror-stricken persons, giving vent to hardly intelligible cries of terror and distress]

Voices

They have broken in at Moria Gate.—All is lost.—My wife.—My children.—God help us.—To the temple.—Elijah, Elijah!—Where shall we hide?—What will become of us?

A Voice

To the walls! Man the walls!

A Man

[Rushing in] We are betrayed! The king has fled! We are lost!

Voices

We are betrayed.—We are lost.—Where is the king?—Where are the priests?—Where is Hananiah?—Revenge, revenge.—Death is upon us.—The Chaldeans.

The Strident Voice

Curses upon the king!

Voices

[Fiercely] Curses upon the king!

The Strident Voice

A curse on the priests! A curse on the prophets! They lied to us one and all.

Voices

Yes, curse them every one!

The Strident Voice

They persecuted those who warned us, those who counseled peace.

A Voice

They persecuted Jeremiah.

A Second Voice

Yes, Jeremiah told us what would happen.

Voices

He warned us.—He wanted peace.—In this very place he shouted for peace.—I heard him.—He is the true prophet.—Everything has happened as he foretold. Where is Jeremiah?—Fetch Jeremiah. He will help us.—Where is he?—Where is he?

A Voice

They have prisoned him in the pit, here in the palace.

[Cries of fury arise from the crowd]

Voices

Set him free.—He will save us.—Force the doors.—Jeremiah, Jeremiah!
God has sent him to help us.—Jeremiah, man of God, come to our aid.—
Down with the false prophets.—God spoke through Jeremiah.—Bring an
axe to force the door.—Jeremiah shall be king.—Where is our saviour?

[For a time nothing can be heard but the cry, Jeremiah, Jeremiah, and the
noise made by the beating of axes and staves upon the door. Suddenly
the door is opened and the doorkeeper appears]

Doorkeeper

What would ye?

The Crowd

Let us pass.—Jeremiah, Jeremiah!

[The Doorkeeper is thrust aside]

Doorkeeper

Help, help!

[Part of the mob disappears through the doorway, and from within is
heard the noise of doors being broken down with axes. Those who
remain on the steps are tense with excitement and impatience]

Voices

[From within] The dogs have lowered him into the pit.—They were afraid
of him.

Voices

[From the steps] He is a holy man.—He is the chosen of the Lord.—
Jeremiah will save us all.

A Woman

[Frenzied with excitement] He stretched forth his hand and cried, Peace. God's fire breathed from his lips. His brow shone like that of an angel. He will save us.

Another Woman

Could I but look upon his blessed face once more. It will shed light over Jerusalem.

[Cries come from within]

Voices

They have found him.—He is saved.—We are saved.—God will help us.—Jeremiah! Jeremiah!

[Reappearing from within, the rest of the crowd brings Jeremiah triumphantly to the top of the steps. He stands with his hand shielding his eyes from the light]

Voices

[Ecstatically] Holy One!—Master!—Samuel.—Elijah.—Prophet.—Save us, Jeremiah.—King.—Anointed of the Lord.—Israel hear his words.—Jeremiah.

The Frenzied Woman

[Throwing herself at his feet] Why do you hide your face? Your glance brings healing. Look on this child of mine that it may grow hale. Look upon us all that we may arise from death.

Jeremiah

[Slowly withdraws his hand from his eyes. His gaze is serious and even gloomy, as he contemplates the agitated and expectant throng] The light is strange to my eyes, and burns them. Strange, too, is this love you show me, and it burns my soul. What would ye?

The Crowd

Save us, Jeremiah, anointed of the Lord.—Save the city.—Be our king.—Show a miracle.

Jeremiah

Your words are dark to me. What is your will?

The Crowd

[All speaking at once] Moria.—The fortress of Zion.—Save Jerusalem.—A miracle.—We are lost.—You are our shepherd.—Save us.—Save Jerusalem.

Jeremiah

Speak one at a time.

The Woman

[Again throwing herself at his feet] Holy One, anointed of the Lord, star of our hope! Stretch forth your hand and save Jerusalem. What you foretold hath been fulfilled. The Chaldeans are upon us.

A Voice

They have broken down Moria Gate.

A Second Voice

Our men have been defeated.

A Third Voice

[Despairingly] Save Jerusalem, or we perish.

The Crowd

[Taking up the cry] Save Jerusalem, or we perish.

[Jeremiah stands motionless, hiding his face in his hands]

The Woman

We would take vengeance on your enemies; we would tear the faces of those who have reviled you. Have pity on us, you who are our saviour and our hope.

A Voice

Who shall save us unless it be you?

The Strident Voice

The priests have betrayed us. The king has sold us to the enemy.

Jeremiah

[Indignantly] It is false! Why slander ye the king?

Voices

Zedekiah has forsaken us.—Where is he?—Why does he not come to our help?—He has fled.

Jeremiah

[Vehemently] It is not true.

Voices

It is true.—They led us into this war.—They have sacrificed us.—We wanted peace.—Let us have peace.

Jeremiah

Tardily comes your longing for peace. Why do ye put your transgressions on the king's shoulders? Ye clamored for war.

The Crowd

No, not I.—No, not I.—It was the king.—Not I.—Not one of us.

Jeremiah

Ye all wanted war, all, all! Your hearts are fickle, and ye sway in the wind like reeds. The very ones who now shout for peace, I have heard howling for war. Those who raise their voices against the king, hounded him on to the fray. Woe unto you, O people! Ye speak with two voices, and drive before every breeze. Ye have fornicated with war, and shall now bear the fruit of war. Ye have played with the sword, and shall now taste its edge.

Voices

Alas, he spurns us.—Jeremiah, be merciful to us in our distress.—Aid us in our wretchedness.

Jeremiah

No man can help you. Help cometh from God alone.

The Strident Voice

God has forsaken us.

The Crowd

Yea, God has forsaken us.—Where is he?—Where is the covenant?

Fugitives

[Rush past shouting] The enemy is within the gates. Abimelech is slain.

The Crowd

[Shrieks with terror, and then appeals once more to Jeremiah] Hearken, hearken!—We are lost!—Show a miracle, a miracle.

Jeremiah

[Despairingly] What would ye that I should do? Am I to stretch forth my bare hands against the enemy?

The Crowd

[Ecstatically] Yea, yea; that do, and save us.

Jeremiah

Think ye then that I can drive back those whom God sendeth against you?

The Crowd

Yea, yea.—You can.—You must.—You can do what you will.

Jeremiah

Naught can I do. Naught against the will of God.

The Crowd

You can save Jerusalem.—Show a miracle.

Jeremiah

[Fiercely] Were it in my power to work against God's will, verily I would not do so. Tempt me not. I am on God's side, not on yours. Whatever he decrees, I bow myself before him.

Voices

Alas, he spurns us.—He forsakes us.

Jeremiah

[In growing excitement] To him, whose purposes are fixed, do I cling, spurning you, fickle ones. Not your will be done, but his. Whatever thy will, Lord, I submit. Let Jerusalem perish, so it be thy will, I submit. [Cries of horror from the crowd] Let thy temple fall, so it be thy will, I submit. [The crowd bursts into furious exclamations] Let the towers crash, let thy people be scattered like dust and its very name vanish from the earth, let my body be given over to shame and my soul to torment, so it be thy will, I submit, Lord, I submit.

The Crowd

He raves.—Strike him down.—He is mad.—He rains curses on us.—Silence the traitor!

Jeremiah

[In a trance] Whatsoever thou doest, Lord, I submit.
Whatsoever thou sendest, I glorify thy name.
Rain down on me terrors uncounted,
Thine anger I welcome, I seek not to hide.
Break my heart! Burst the gates! Raze the walls!
With fire consume thine own altar,
To defend which now myriads fall!
Rejecting thy people, the chosen,
Turn thy face from me too in thy wrath!
From the depth of my sorrow I cling to thee;

Though thou slay me, I trust thee in death.

The Crowd

[Shouting fiercely] Traitor.—He is cursing us.—He prays for our death. Stone him.—Stone him!

Jeremiah

[More frenzied than ever, as he daunts the menacing and turbulent mob with the fire of his enthusiasm]

Not my will, Lord, but thine be done!
Thou hast led me into darkness;
I have known many afflictions;
Lord, I will bear all patiently.
Pour out the vials of thine anger,
Break my bones, close mine eyes,
Fill up the measure of my sufferings,
Pressed down and running over,
Still am I thy faithful servant,
For art not thou the Most High?
The more thou visitest me with wormwood and gall,
The more will I testify to thine abounding love.
Let me double the martyrdom thou wouldst impose,
Let me kiss the rod that striketh the blows,
Let me thank the hand that bruiseth my flesh,
Let me praise the brand that seareth my flesh,
Let me bless the death wrought by foes without pity,
Let me bless the destruction befallen thy city,
Let me bless bitterness, slavery, shame,
Let me bless the enemy, bless in thy name.
Lord to thy wishes I humbly bow!
To accept all thy sendings I fervently vow!
Lord, hear my words; Lord, prove me now!

The Crowd

[Cutting him short] Traitor.—Stone him.—He blesses our foes.—He prays for our enemies.—Stone the blasphemer, stone him.

The Strident Voice
[Dominating the rest] Crucify him! Crucify him!

The Crowd
[Echoing the cry and rushing up the steps] Crucify him! Nail the blasphemer to the cross.—Stone the traitor.—Crucify him!

Jeremiah
[In ecstasy, stretching out his arms as if on the cross]
Let God's will be done. Come hither, draw near,
Nail my limbs to the cross, pierce my side with the spear,
Spit upon me, and scourge and revile me,
Break my bones, and debase and defile me,
Thus shall I be, for one and for all,
A trespass offering made for Israel!
Seize me, then, seize;
Let my sacrifice please
Jehovah, his anger yet stem;
And save, even now, save Jerusalem.

[The crowd surges round him. Some grasp his limbs, while others strive on his behalf and endeavor to free him]

Voices
Crucify him!—Stone him!—He blasphemes.—A curse upon Jeremiah!—Crucify him.

Other Voices
Let be.—The spirit of God is upon him.—He is beside himself.—Harm him not.

Jeremiah
[Amid the tumult he continues to stretch out his arms as if on the cross]
But why do ye tarry? Thrice-blessed day!
The price of martyrdom fain would I pay.

For suffering I am athirst.
Let me die the death accurst.
Who hangs on the cross in mortal pain,
The world's eternal welfare shall gain,
Saviour and intercessor, he,
With arms outstretched on the cruel tree.
His lips, trembling with anguish till death bring release,
Shall speak the redeeming message of peace;
His sighs to melody shall give birth,
His torment, to love everlasting on earth.
His death shall bring life; his sorrows, forgiveness.
Though his flesh know corruption, his body decay,
Yet his soul, winging heavenward,
Beareth all our sins Godward,
The glorious messenger, he, of man's new day!
Ah, were I but that herald of deliverance!
My spirit is on fire! Lo, I pray:
Crucify me, oh, crucify me!

[With wild cries they seize him, and begin to carry him away, buffeting him as they go]

Voices

Crucify him!—Let him taste the death he yearns for.—He is our enemy.—Crucify him.—Stone him!

[At this moment a number of fugitives rush into the marketplace in wild disorder, throwing away their weapons as they run]

Fugitives

The walls are down.—The enemy is in the city. The Chaldeans have gained the day.—Israel is lost.

More Fugitives

Abimelech is slain.—All is lost.—Jerusalem is fallen.

Yet More Fugitives

[In full flight] They are hard on our heels.—To the temple.—All is lost.—
Israel! Israel.—Alas for Jerusalem.

[The crowd joins the fugitives, uttering shrieks of terror. Jeremiah is
forgotten. The whole city seems to ring with cries of despair and the
noise of vain attempts at flight]

THE CONVERSION

SCENE EIGHT

My desire is that Job may be tried unto the end. Job XXXIV, 36.

SCENE EIGHT

A vast crypt with shutters and doors closed so that the damp
underground space is but dimly lighted. Fugitives, wan and careworn,
are crouching and lying on the stone flooring. Some of them have
gathered round an elder who is reading from the scriptures. In the
background lies a wounded man, tended by a woman. Remote from the
rest, sitting on a piece of masonry, and as motionless as if he were
himself carved out of the rock, is Jeremiah, his face buried in his hands.
He plays no part in what is going on, so that his silence is as it were a
rock fixed in the current of plaints and disputes. It is evening, on the day
after the taking of Jerusalem. As the elder reads, he sways his body
rhythmically in time to the words, which are low and monotonous,
except when he raises his voice to express despair or hope. From time to
time, the others take up the responses.

The Elder
[Reading]
Give ear, O Shepherd of Israel,
Thou that leadest Joseph like a flock;
Thou that dwellest between the cherubims,
Shine forth! Stir up thy strength!

The Others
[Murmuring in unison] Shine forth! Stir up thy strength!

The Elder
[Reading]
Give ear, O Shepherd, come and save us.
Cause thy face to shine, and we shall be saved.
How long wilt thou be angry against the prayer of thy people?
Thou feedest them with the bread of tears,
And givest them tears to drink in great measure.
O God of hosts,
Cause thy face to shine, and we shall be saved.

The Others
Cause thy face to shine, and we shall be saved.

The Elder
[Reading]
O remember not against us former iniquities;
Let thy tender mercies speedily prevent us:
For we are brought very low.
We are consumed by thine anger,
And by thy wrath we are troubled.
Remember not against us our former iniquities.
Remember thy covenant, remember thy name.
Appear, Shepherd, lead thy flock home;
Shine forth! Stir up thy strength!

The Others
Shine forth! Stir up thy strength!

Other Voices
[Joining in fervently] Cause thy face to shine, and we shall be saved.

The Wounded Man
[Who has hitherto been moaning, now bursts into a loud cry] Oh, oh, I am burning. Water! Water!

The Woman
[Trying to soothe him] Be quiet, there's a good man. For God's sake, be quiet, or they will hear us.

The Elder
Be silent! Control yourself, or you will destroy us all.

Another
They will slay us if they find us.

The Wounded Man

Let them kill me. I cannot bear it. My wound is on fire. Water! Water!

A Man

We must silence him. His cries will betray our hiding place.

The Woman

Touch him not. He is my brother. I bore him hither from the walls. [She kneels beside him] Dear, I implore you to stifle your cries. I will fetch you some water. Take my kerchief and muffle your mouth in it.

[The wounded man does so. His cries fall to a whisper. The others, most of whom have stood up in their excitement, settle down again]

A Voice

Go on reading, Pinchas. God's word consoles us.

Another Voice

Go on reading about the promise.

Other Voices

Yes, read us about the Messiah; about the rod that shall come forth out of the stem of Jesse.—Read about the saviour.—Our hearts are thirsting after the dew of the word.

[The Elder takes up the roll once more, and is about to resume his reading, when there comes a knocking. All start]

A Woman

[Alarmed] Someone knocks!

The Others

They are there!—They have tracked us.

186

A Man

It is not on the outer door, but from the secret entrance, which is known to our own folk alone. Open!

The Women

No! No, there are traitors among us. Let be!

The Elder

Silence! [He cautiously approaches a door hidden among buttresses] Who is there?

Voice

[From without] Zephaniah!

The Elder

It is Zephaniah, my son-in-law, whom we sent forth for news.

[He draws back the bolt, and a man enters, helmeted and garbed like a Chaldean. All rush towards him, Jeremiah alone remaining motionless]

Voices

What has happened?—Have you seen Neter, my son? Tebiah, my wife?— Have they burned down my house?—Where is the king?—What has happened to the temple? Do you know anything about my husband, Ishmael?—What is happening outside?

The Elder

Be silent all. Let Zephaniah speak, for he has seen the daylight and the city.

Zephaniah

Better to sit in darkness than to see what I have seen; better still to weep oneself blind; even better were it to sleep among the roots of the trees and in the bowels of the earth. David's city has become a city of the dead; the citadel of Solomon is utterly destroyed.

All

Alas, alas, for Jerusalem.

Zephaniah

The corpses of our brothers lie like dung in the streets. The Chaldeans are stripping the bodies of the slain; they have rifled the tombs of the kings of Judah; and for the purple vesture of Solomon they have cast lots; they have seized the bread from the holy table; and they have stolen the golden candlesticks from the walls.

The Elder

[Rending his garments] I can live no longer! Could I but tear my bowels as I tear my raiment.

Voices

Where is the power of God?—The covenant.—The promise.—Where are our leaders?—Jerusalem is lost.—My husband?—Whom have you seen?— What has become of Nahum?—What has become of ...

Zephaniah

For many do you ask, and I can give but one answer for them all. Of the nobles of Judah, not one now looketh on the light of day.

Voices

All slain? All?—Impossible!—Abodassar?—Jehoiachin?—Hedassar?—Imre? —Nahum?

Zephaniah

Ask me no more. Their troubles are over, and they are with God.

Voices

Nahum too?—The king's sons?—My brother-in-law Absalom?

Zephaniah

None are left alive. Those who fell not at the wall were slain afterwards by Nebuchadnezzar's officers. Zedekiah alone remains.

Voices

Zedekiah still alive?—Why spare him more than another?—He has betrayed us.—Why show him mercy when all the rest have been butchered?—Why spare him?

Zephaniah

Honor the king! Reverence his sufferings.

Voices

What has happened to him?—Is he a prisoner?

Zephaniah

Zedekiah forced his way through, with sixty of the bravest who hoped to renew the struggle against Ashur in the hills. But the army of the Chaldeans pursued him and overtook him in the plains, and carried him to King Nebuchadnezzar.

Voices

And then?

Zephaniah

My path crossed his. I saw him in the square bound with fetters of brass. Before his eyes, one by one, his sons were put to the sword. Then came it to pass that the anointed of the Lord was blinded ...

Jeremiah

[Suddenly roused from his impassivity and speaking in horror-stricken tones] Blinded, you say? Blinded?

Zephaniah

Who is this?

Voices

Do not speak to him.—Do not look at him.—He is the most infamous of men.—A curse lies on him.—Utter not his name.—Utter not his name.

Zephaniah

Who is it that spake, saying "Blinded?" I am sure I know the voice.

Voices

Ask not his name.—He is one accurst.—He is rejected of God.

A Woman

He is the curse of God, sent for our burning torment. He is the scourge of God.—Jeremiah, Jeremiah!

Zephaniah

[With a wild outcry, stretching forth his hands as if to thrust away something horrible] Jeremiah!

Jeremiah

Why do you shrink from me? What are you afraid of? There is no longer any reason for fear. My words were but wind; my force is spent. Spew me out, and go on your way.

Zephaniah

I tremble before you, man of doom.—He foresaw everything. He alone. That other called on his name.

The Elder

Who called on his name?

Zephaniah

[Utterly crushed] Zedekiah, the king. They brought him in chains, held him fast lest he should turn away his head, forced him to watch the slaughter of his sons. Fain would he have made no complaint. He bit his lip and was silent as the first fell. But when they seized the second, he moved as if to speak. As the third was struck down, a word escaped from his mouth. Not a plea for mercy. He cried, "Jeremiah, Jeremiah."

[All shudder]

Thus in his anguish he called upon Jeremiah. When the fiery steel pierced his eyes, again did he call on the name of Jeremiah, saying: "Jeremiah, Jeremiah, where art thou, revealer? Where art thou, Jeremiah, my brother?" Zedekiah called upon his name, the name of him who had foreseen.

[They shrink away from Jeremiah, as from a dangerous beast]

Jeremiah

[Struggling with emotion] It is false. Not by my will did this happen. Let him not dare to accuse me. The word came to me; what I said was struck from me as we strike fire from flint. I wished him no ill. God made me a liar, resist his power as I would. Not mine the will that moved me.

Zephaniah

What is he talking about?

A Woman

Madness hath seized him.

Another Woman

He raves.

A Man

Nay, he foretold these happenings. A sage is he, and a prophet.

Jeremiah

Why should the king accuse me? A greater power than mine constrained my utterance. I was the tool of the pitiless one, his breath, the slave of his malice. He commanded, and I had to obey, for his strength is greater than mine. He breathed curses into my breath. His was the gall in my speech, his the bitterness in my spittle. Woe upon the hands of God; whom he seizes, shall not again be loosed. Ah, would he but set me free from his curse, that no longer I might have to speak his words. [A pause] No longer will I speak his words. I will hold my peace. [A pause] God! No longer will I obey thy behests. I curse thy curses. Lift thy hand from me, take the fire from my mouth. No more can I bear.

Voices

He is in a frenzy.—Look how convulsions rack him.—He is twisted with pain like a woman in labour.—Heed not his words.—God has punished him.

[Jeremiah sinks to the ground broken]

Look, look, the hand of the Lord hath fallen upon him.—Go not near him whom God hath banned.

[They draw farther away from Jeremiah and huddle together. Jeremiah lies like a felled tree. For a few moments there is a hush of despair. This silence is broken by the sound of a distant trumpet]

Zephaniah

Alas, they draw near, the heralds of disaster.

The Crowd

[To Zephaniah] What is it?—What has happened?—What meaneth this summons?

Zephaniah

'Tis Nebuchadnezzar's message to the remnant of the people.

Voices

Must we go forth to hear the message?—Dare we leave our shelter?—What shall we do, Zephaniah?

Zephaniah

No need for haste. Evil tidings ever come too soon.

Voices

What is to happen?—What is our doom?

Zephaniah

It is the will of Nebuchadnezzar that our city be utterly destroyed.

[There is a wail of horror. The trumpet is heard once more, nearer]

Those who survive must go as slaves to Babylon.

Voices

We are to leave Zion?

The Elder

I will not go. Here will I remain.

Zephaniah

Who refuses to go, shall perish by the sword. All are to make ready for the journey and are to assemble in the marketplace. Thrice at dawning will the trumpet sound. Thereafter, anyone who lingers in the city, is to be slain.

The Elder

Let death come! I will not go. There is no life for me away from Jerusalem. The grave is better than slavery in a far country.

A Woman

My brother, my nephew, and my husband have all been slain. Tombs are my heritage, and this heritage will I keep.

A Man

I shall stay! I shall stay! Here have I struck my roots, and from this soil alone can I draw strength. Palsied would be my arm should I try to plough the furrow in another land, and my eyes would not serve me in a strange world.

Voices

[In the enthusiasm of despair] Let us stay.—Let us choose death.—Better death than slavery.—Never will we go into exile.—Better to die.

The Wounded Man

[Half rising] No, no.—Not death for me. Life is what I crave. Exile is better than death. I cannot walk, and if ye stay who will carry me? Do not forsake me. Life, life!

His Sister

Be calm. I will carry you.

The Wounded Man

[Deliriously] Yes ... Let us go. Let us leave these mad folk, who want to die. Why should we seek death?

The Elder

His body is parched with fever. He knows not what he says.

The Wounded Man

[Fiercely] I know, I know. I have been near to death, and would rather live than die. Better to burn, better to suffer, than to feel nothing at all. While there is life there is hope.

A Young Woman

True, true! I too want to live. My life lies before me. As yet I have seen nothing, felt nothing. Young and vigorous are my limbs. Death is cold, life is warm. I will not stay. I will go with you, anywhere, anywhere.

Another Woman

Shameless one, are you willing to be the concubine of an enemy?

The Young Woman

Anything, if I can but live.

The Wounded Man

Life, at any cost of suffering.

A Man

[Wildly] No life without God! No life without Jerusalem!

Voices

Death were better.—Death were better.—Let us not accept slavery.—
Death is a fearful thing.

[Again the trumpet sounds, now close at hand]

A Voice

Let them call, I will not hearken. I hear the voice of death, loud and clear like the voice of God. We must not heed the lure. Better to perish with Jerusalem.

The Elder

I hold thee fast, city of Zion. Weak though my hands, still do I cling to thee. My life hast thou been, be also my death. How could I breathe without thee, how open my eyes in the morning without being able to look upon Solomon's house and God's dwelling. Rather would I be buried in thy earth than walk at large in another land; rather would I lie dead with my fathers than live to be the slave of the heathen. Jerusalem, Jerusalem, Jerusalem, take me to thy bosom. As I have been with thee in life, let me be with thee in death.

Zephaniah

In this you and I must part company. Death has no charms for me. I have seen too many dead lying in the streets, and I tell you that life is better.

The Wounded Man

[Raising himself] Yea, let me live, to feel but a grain of sand between my fingers. To look again upon the almond blossoms, to see them open as night falls. To watch the moon waxing and waning in its passage across the starry heavens. Even if life were to deny all its joys, even if I were to be crippled and deaf, yet still might I look upon the glorious things in the world, still draw the breath of life. Let me feel my heart beating, the warm blood coursing through my veins. Give me life, I ask nothing more!

The Elder

Shame upon you, weaklings! Would you live without God?

Voices

God will be with us wherever we go.—God speaks to us wherever we may be.—Even from exile our voices will rise towards him.—There too shall we be faithful. The light of his countenance shines upon all roads.

The Elder

Nay, nay, who leaveth Jerusalem, leaveth God behind. Here and here only is the dwelling of Jehovah. Sacrifice at any other altar than this can be naught but idolatry.

Voices

[In conflict] No.—Yes.—God is everywhere.—He is here only.—He will reveal himself to us anywhere.—God abides nowhere but in his own temple.—Anywhere, everywhere.—Nowhere but in Jerusalem can we look upon his face.

Jeremiah

[Suddenly springing to his feet, with an awesome outburst] God is nowhere! Nowhere at all! Who among the living hath seen him, who hath heard the sound of his voice? Those who seek him, seek him in vain; those who created him, lied before the faces of men. God is nowhere! Neither in heaven, nor on earth, nor in the souls of men.

The Elder

[His jaw has dropped in amazement and horror. At length he raises his hands tremblingly towards heaven, with the invocation] Blasphemy! Blasphemy! Strike him down with thy lightnings.

Jeremiah

[More fiercely] Who hath blasphemed him, if it be not God himself? He hath broken his covenant, thrown down his walls, and burned his own temple. He denies himself; he himself blasphemes God; he and none other!

The Elder
Heed him not! A backslider is he, and an outcast. Heed him not, ye servants of the Almighty.

Jeremiah
[Still more fiercely] Who has served him in Israel as I have served him? Who within Jerusalem's walls has been more faithful than I? For his sake I left my home; for his sake I refused to comfort my mother in death. I have sacrificed friendship to him, and for his jealousy have I forfeited the love of women. I have submitted to his will as a wife submits to her husband. The words that I spake were those which he put into my mouth; his was the blood in my body; my thoughts were the children of his will; his were the dreams that visited my sleep. I gave my back to the smiters; I hid not my face from shame and spitting. I served him, I served him, for I believed that through me he would avert the evil to come. I cursed, thinking he would turn my curses into blessings. I prophesied, thinking he would prove me a liar, would save Jerusalem. But my prophecies have been fulfilled, and God is proved a liar. Woe is me that I served the faithless one so faithfully! He sent me that my brothers should laugh me to scorn while I spat upon their joys. Now, when misery has befallen them, he wishes that I in turn should mock their distress. But I do not laugh, God! I will not laugh at my brothers' torment. Not like thee can I rejoice at another's sorrow. The odor of the slaughter-house delights not my nostrils. Too harsh for me is thy harshness, too heavy thy hand! No longer will I be the instrument of thy vengeance; no longer will I serve thee. I tear asunder the bond between thee and me. I tear it asunder!

Voices
He raves.—He blasphemes.—Away with him.—He is beside himself.

Jeremiah
[In an ecstasy, speaks over their heads into the void]
Dumb and sinister Being, I witness against thee!
Be thou silent no longer, witness thou against me!
Say,
Have I ever, I charge thee, proved backward or loath?
Have I ever, I charge thee, been false to my oath?
Dumb and sinister Being, thy silence now break.
Ope thy mouth, and against me thy parable take.

Thou hast sought me by day and by night and hast found me,
With dreams to amaze, and with fears to confound me.
With fire my soul thou hast filled. As a brand
Spreading flame, spreading flame far and wide through the land,
Hast thou driven me on. 'Twas thy will not mine,
Made me stand as a foe 'gainst this people of thine.
I was the hand their throats fiercely clamping,
I was the hoof, their peace roughly down stamping,
I was the saw, their limbs ever rending,
I was the goad, bringing torment unending,
I was the terror, the vision of fright,
I was the nightmare that rode them by night.
In their bones I the fire, in their flesh I the thorn,
The mockery, likewise, that laughed them to scorn;
For relentless, unfeeling, as any dumb beast,
Made mad by thy will, I obeyed thy behest.
Of the love of my brothers though still I was fain,
Made mad by thy will, I but cursed them again.
Thus quelling compassion, constrained to do ill,
I spurred myself onward thy word to fulfil.

Voices

He is seized with the frenzy of fever.—He raves.—To whom is he
speaking?—He is out of his wits.

Jeremiah

But I renounce my allegiance!
Resuming my freedom, no longer a thrall,
I nor heed thy commandments nor answer thy call!
Where 'twas shrined in my heart I thy image discrown,
And from out thy high heaven I hurl thee adown!
Thou spurnedst thy people, so thee too I reject;
No merciless God shall compel my respect!
For why is it seemly that reverence be paid
To a god who gives scorn when his children seek aid?
He only is God who turns sorrow aside,
Almighty but he who can solace provide!

198

And of men him alone may we prophet proclaim
Whose spirit with measureless love is aflame,
Whose words and whose deeds teach all men to know
That his soul with compassion is ever aglow.
Now to me my purpose in life is plain,
For the plaints that assail thine ears all in vain
Wring my heart with the passion of infinite pain.
Come cries from the city thine anger hath burned,
Come cries from the people thy hatred hath spurned,
Come cries from the widows, made widows by thee,
Come cries from the mothers, made childless by thee,
From the king, now blind, as by thee ordained,
From thine altar, by thine own self profaned;
From the earth, from the air, the message is sent;
As I hearken, with anguish my bowels are rent;
Appeals from the living, appeals from the dead;
As I hearken, perforce I must turn my head
From thee, who art cold and unfeeling as stone,
From thee, who art deaf when thy children make moan,
To my brothers, my sisters, who are bone of my bone
And flesh of my flesh, those whom sorrows invest,
Those whom torments afflict. With them, none but them,
Can my spirit find peace or my heart be at rest.
In reverence I bow before them, none but them;
For them, tenderest love; for thee, God, naught but hate!

The Elder

He hath cursed God. Strike him down.

Voices

He raves.—He is mad.—He dreams.—'Tis dangerous to listen to him.—
Silence the madman!

Jeremiah

[Suddenly kneels and apostrophizes the others]
My brothers, my brothers, forgive me, forgive
The vain pride of a man now unfitted to live!

For God, none but he, with dreams dazzled my eyes.
With words he confused me, with signs led astray,
Until, to an evil self-will giving way,
I believed myself prophet, all-knowing, all-wise!
I believed myself great with the greatness of God,
When, invoking his name, your dooms I shrilled.
When with his curses my mouth was filled!
But lo, I abjure him, this pitiless God!
Though toward you I proved myself arrogant, vain,
I beseech you, my brothers, show mercy again.
Though my curses rained down on you many a day,
Repulse me not now—for he led me astray.
There is naught but forgiveness my spirit to heal;
At your feet now abased, craving pardon, I kneel.

[All draw away from him in horror. He moves after them,
without rising from his knees]

My brothers, my brothers, look kindly on me!
Well assured is my heart that we brothers be,
And I the least worthy, the youngest of all!
Lo, I curse you no longer, but breathe benediction,
Lo, I yearn to share with you the bread of affliction!
Let it please you, my brothers, whate'er may befall,
That I love you, that thanks to the love I bear,
No more word of mine, I swear it, I swear,
Shall add by one grain to your load of care.
In atonement for wrongdoing ask what you will.
The meanest of services glad to fulfil,
As the slave of your slaves I demand only this,
That the dust from your shoes I may thankfully kiss.
My brothers in darkness, my brothers in grief,
From my humble repentance withhold not belief.
My brothers, my brothers, your pardon were bliss.

The Elder
Death to the man who touches him! God hath judged him.

Voices
Accursed of God, away.—Forth from among us.—Poison us no longer with thy presence.—Away liar, away!

Jeremiah
[When they thrust him from them, cries plaintively] Driven out like a leper! [He falls prone]

[There is a peremptory knocking, at the door]

Voices
The heralds!—The Chaldeans!—They knock like masters.—It is not one of our own people. [The knocking becomes more imperative] What impatience!—We must not anger him.—Do not unbar the door, for they are all robbers, the Chaldeans.—We must open to him, or he will grow angry.

The Elder
I will open the door. In the midst of life we are in death.

[He cautiously begins to open the great door, but as soon as the bar is down one of the leaves is violently pushed open and Baruch rushes in. The Elder rebars the door]

Baruch
[His face working with anxiety] Brothers, is Jeremiah here?

The Elder
Name him not! Speak not to him.

Baruch
[Looking around] Jeremiah, Jeremiah!

Jeremiah

[Slowly rising, stares at Baruch as if he were a stranger] Who still seeks me? Who now would tempt me?

Baruch

Master mine, do you not know me? Do you not recognize my voice?

Jeremiah

I will look no more and listen no more. Away, you who still breathe the breath of life! Let me lie and rot!

Baruch

Jeremiah, beloved master, I implore you to collect yourself. The enemy is hunting for you.

Jeremiah

Who still seeks me in this world?

Baruch

You have been betrayed; they know your hiding-place. Nebuchadnezzar has sent officers in search of you.

Jeremiah

Let them come! Blessed be the slayers! Blessed be death!

Baruch

Jeremiah, if you love me, seek refuge in flight. I cannot bear that your life should be forfeited.

Jeremiah

No more love have I for anyone.

Baruch

[Embracing him] Nay, master, my blood rather than yours. I will die with you.

[Violent blows are struck on the door]

The Crowd

[Scattering into the darkest corners] Alas, alas.—The Chaldeans.—Our hour has come.—Jeremiah has brought disaster upon us.—Let us deliver him up.

Baruch

Too late! They are already here.

Jeremiah

Open to them, Baruch. [Baruch hesitates. Jeremiah standing erect speaks slowly and clearly, almost exultantly] Open, that I may receive them. My soul yearns for death. Welcome, first fulfiller of my word! Welcome, Death. Open, Baruch! Open to the deliverer. [Baruch moves to the door where he again hesitates. The door is once more shaken by violent blows from without. Jeremiah repeats masterfully] Open, Baruch, I command you.

[Baruch veils his face and unbars the door. The two leaves of the folding door are flung open, and a gleam of the fading light of evening penetrates the dark crypt. The king's three officers enter, richly apparelled, their figures showing in strong relief against the red sky. Jeremiah stands alone, confronting them]

The Chief Officer

[Advancing to the front] Is the man named Jeremiah among you, the son of Hilkiah of Anathoth?

Jeremiah

I am he whom you seek. Fulfil your orders.

[The Chief Officer prostrates himself before Jeremiah, touching the ground three times with his forehead. The two other officers do the same. Jeremiah, startled, draws back a pace. The Chief Officer rises to his knees]

The Chief Officer

Hail to the interpreter of signs! Honor and glory to the revealer of events, to the seer of that which is hidden. [Having again abased himself three times, he stands erect; his companions follow his example. Jeremiah, recovering composure, regards him gloomily] I bear a message through my unworthy mouth from Nebuchadnezzar, my master, king of kings, destroyer of nations. Thus saith my dread lord. It hath been reported to Nebuchadnezzar that thou alone among thy people foretoldest destruction to the rebels and disgrace to those who goaded on the people to revolt. Melted like lead are the words of the priests who withstood thy strength; but thy warning, like gold, hath endured the test of time. Thy fame hath reached the ears of Nebuchadnezzar, and now he is eager to set eyes upon thee. He sendeth thee raiment such as is worn by the princes of Chaldea, and will have thee for the chief among his servants who wait at his table.

Jeremiah

No more will I serve any, either in heaven above or in the earth beneath, for I have served God and have wearied of that service. Say unto Nebuchadnezzar that I refuse to serve him.

The Chief Officer

Thou understandest not the words of my lord and master. Not to any menial service doth he appoint thee, but would have thee to be the chief over all his servants. Master of the magicians, astrologers, and soothsayers, shalt thou be, reading the stars and foretelling that which is to come. Second to none shalt thou be, but shalt come and go in the palace even as thou wilt.

Jeremiah

I hear your words, and therefrom I learn the king's wishes. Great is the call of Nebuchadnezzar, but greater is the need of mine own people. Hearken, therefore! I enter not the palace where the daughters of Israel will scour the steps as bondwomen. No bread do I break as guest at the table of him who hath profaned the temple of Zion. Not for me the favors of the cruel, nor the grace of him who hath been pitiless.

The Chief Officer

The message I brought thee was a king's message, and to kings obedience is due.

Jeremiah

You brought me true word from Nebuchadnezzar. Render him my answer no less truly. Return to him who sent you, and say unto him: "Thus saith Jeremiah to Nebuchadnezzar. My bitterness has no sweetness for thee, nor shall my lips minister to thy pride. Wert thou to summon me with the tongues of angels, yet would I not heed thy call; wert thou to load for me with gold all the stones of Jerusalem, yet would I not speak soft words to thee. Honor me if you wilt, to thee I pay not honor. Seek me if thou wilt, but thee I will not seek."

The Chief Officer

Bethink thee, 'tis the king of kings who summons thee to enjoy the light of his countenance.

Jeremiah

I refuse to go! I refuse!

The Chief Officer

Never before hath any man refused to comply with the wishes of Nebuchadnezzar.

Jeremiah

Nevertheless I refuse, I, the least among the sons of Israel. Who is he, that I should fear him? His power is but a straw, and his wrath but a breath of wind.

The Chief Officer

Rash and presumptuous art thou, to speak thus lightly of the king my master. Curb thy tongue, and have a care for thy life.

Jeremiah

[Fiercely] Who is he that I should fear him? Many have there been who bore the proud name of Pharaoh, many whose foreheads were once adorned with circlets of gold, but no man careth to remember their deeds, and no man taketh pen to inscribe their names in the book of time. There have been mightier than he, whom the generations of men have forgotten ere the trees they planted have rotted. Who is Nebuchadnezzar under the stars, that I should fear him? Is he not a worm, even as other men? Does not death dog his footsteps, and corruption await his body? Shall he escape the finger of time? Think you that he, more than another, can keep that which he now hath, or that he can find an issue from the doom which awaits all the sons of men? Return, therefore, to your master, bearing from me this message: "Woe to the destroyer, for he shall be destroyed! Woe to the robber, for he shall be robbed. He who has drunk his fill of blood, shall be drowned in blood; he who has battened on the flesh of the nations, shall himself soon become food for worms! Hearken! A wind is rising against Babylon, and a tempest is about to break over Nineveh! Numbered are the days of Ashur. Drawn is the sword, and it hangs over thee, thy people, and thy realm. Thou art greedy for news of that which is to come. Learn, O Nebuchadnezzar, that Ashur is ripe for destruction; the measure of thine iniquity is full."

[The officers shrink before these fiery words, and make gestures as if to avert the threatened doom]

The Elder
[Suddenly stands forth from a dark corner, and cries enthusiastically]
Hear him, O Lord, hear him! Fulfil the promise of his words.

Voices
[Imploringly] Hear him, Lord God of Sabaoth!

Jeremiah
Already hath the avenger awakened, for the Lord hath summoned him, and hath equipped him with strength. He is coming. Already is he near. Mighty are his hands; they will crush Babylon like a bird's nest, and will scatter the people of Ashur like chaff before the wind. Set watchmen in the towers upon the walls, that they may warn you of his coming; send forth men in armor, bearing sharp spears, that they may resist his onslaught. Just as little as thou canst blow away the clouds of heaven with thy breath, just so little canst thou avert the coming of the avenger, whose sword will slay the children of Ashur.

The Elder

[Ecstatically] So let it be, Lord, so let it be!

The Other Refugees

[They have collected round The Elder, and have caught fire from his enthusiasm] Smite them, O Lord, as he has foretold.—Fulfil the words he has spoken.—Send the avenger.—Cast down Babylon even as he has prophesied.—Hear him, O Lord, hear him.

[The officers, panic-stricken, make for the door]

Jeremiah

[In a frenzy of joy] O fool among fools, didst thou verily believe thou couldst enslave us; didst thou verily believe that God would forget us, would forsake his city of Jerusalem? Are we not his children, his first-born and his heirs? Is not his spirit upon us, and his blessing upon the seed of Abraham? He has chastised us for our sins, but will now have pity on us. What his left hand has taken from us, his right hand will restore a thousandfold. For know, brothers, that sooner shall mountains fall and rivers flow upwards, sooner shall the stars be darkened, than that God shall forget his covenant, shall abandon Israel, shall turn away his face from Zion.

[The officers have vanished during this speech]

The Elder and The Others

[Thronging round Jeremiah] Blessings upon your words.—Blessings upon your head.—God will be mindful of Jerusalem.—O glorious prophecy!

Jeremiah

[Ignoring them in his growing exaltation] How dark were the days upon earth when God frowned upon his children. We thought to perish in that darkness, to go down unto death in our anguish. But with the end of his wrath came the beginning of his love. A storm has raged; God has broken our strength like a reed. But now, once more, the sun of his mercy shines upon us. He has laid aside the lightnings; he has stilled the thunder of his voice; his words fall softly on our ears. Sweet do they sound, sweet and gentle:

Arise, Jerusalem,
Arise, city of affliction.
Fear no longer,
For I have compassion upon thee.
I have been wroth with thee,
For a moment I have forsaken thee,
But not for ever doth mine anger endure.
Therefore, since thou hast been forsaken,
Hast been for a day the rejected of God,
Now shall thy glories be restored unto thee,
And now shalt thou be exalted for all eternity.
I will deck thee with my love,
And girdle thee with peace,
Will show thee the light of my countenance,
And bestow my blessing upon thee.
Arise, Jerusalem,
Arise,
For I have delivered thee.

The Elder

A blessing upon your words.

The Others

Hear him, God.—Fulfil his words.—Deliver Jerusalem.

Jeremiah

Lo, she is risen. She has heard the call. The Lord has loosened the fetters from her limbs, and has lifted the yoke from her neck. He has wiped the tears from her cheeks, has consoled the widows and the orphans. Smiles succeed to sorrow. The season of blossoming hath returned. Zion yearns for her children, that they may look upon her in her happiness and rejoice in her renewal. Already have the children of Israel heard the summons of the Lord. Dispersed never so widely to the ends of the earth and among the islands of the sea, yet do they return in their myriads to Zion. From the north and the south, from the east and the west, the happy pilgrims come. Their footsteps hasten across the hills of Gilead, eagerly do they make their way over Bashan and Carmel, that they may see the city of our love, the city of our suffering, the holy fortress of Zion. And Jerusalem rejoices to welcome her children, returned in countless numbers from the prison-houses of exile. Where the flowers were withered, new buds are springing; where darkness had loomed, there shines fresh light; those who have been dumb, find voice. Jerusalem has risen from the tomb. The hills nod to her as of old; the shadows of the mountains lie athwart her plains; as dew gleams in the meadows, so peace shines in the city, the peace of the Lord, the peace of Israel, the peace of Jerusalem!

The Others

Fulfil the prophecy, O God.—Bring peace to Israel.—Let Jerusalem arise.

Jeremiah

When the glad day comes, and in Zion we meet,
We, who so long have been captives and slaves,
Who have dwelt with the stranger in gloomy abodes,
Joyfully reassembling,
We shall pray:
Blessed be thy name, Lord God of Sabaoth!
Great and wonderful have been thy mercies!
By the waters of Babylon we sat down and wept,
Breaking the bitter bread of slavery;
We mingled the wine in our pitchers with tears;
For our souls were sick with longing for home,
And our servitude was a daily death.
Then we called unto thee, compassionate one, and called not in vain,
For thou didst break our bonds.
With the dew of thy goodness, with the waters of life,
Didst thou quench the fever of our thirsty souls.
Us the dispersed, us the vanquished,
Didst thou raise from the dust and lead home to Zion.
Look on us, O mountains; look on us, O fields!
We have returned, we have risen as from the dead!
Let the sound of our streamlets murmur in our prayers;
Let the gardens welcome us with their flowers;
Let the roses of Sharon greet us with their perfume,

The forests of Carmel and Lebanon with their shade.
And thou, holy city, the beloved, ne'er forgotten,
The vision of our days, and the dream of our nights,
The bride of our love and the mother of us all,
Let thy cymbals sound, thy flutes breathe notes of gladness;
Arouse thee and give utterance to thy rejoicing,
For we have returned to thee, Jerusalem!

The Others
[Pressing near him in their delight, throwing themselves at his feet, embracing his knees] Returned!—Risen as from the dead.—Glorious prophecy.—Jerusalem.—Jerusalem.

Baruch
[On his knees] My master, my teacher, how sweet are your words, how blissful is your message.

The Elder
Blessed be he who brings comfort in time of affliction.

A Woman
His eyes glow like stars and light up the vault.

Another Woman
God's spirit has descended on him.

The Wounded Man
His words have heartened me. I live, I live again. Oh that I, too, might one day return to Jerusalem.

Zephaniah
Your words have brought me new courage, Jeremiah.

Jeremiah
[Paying no heed, but gradually awakening from his trance and looking round with alarm] Where are they to whom I spake? Surely I talked with

messengers from King Nebuchadnezzar? Have I been dreaming? Methought there were three men, richly appareled.

The Elder
They fled before the lightnings of your glance.

Another
Your anger smote them like a sword.

Jeremiah
[Still confused] What did I say? My mind is dark, and yet I seem to recall something. What did I say? Why do you all look at me yearningly? Why do you crowd round me? You looked at me with horror in your faces, but now ... What has happened to me, and what has happened to you?

The Elder
Man of God, man into whose heart the fire of God has passed, this light streams from you. Mightily have you prophesied to us.

A Man
You have freed my soul from its anguish.

A Woman
You have feasted my heart on manna.

The Wounded Man
Look at me. I can get up. I can walk. The pain has gone. Your words have called me back from death.

Voices
A miracle.—A miracle like those of Elijah.—Raising from the dead.—Let us bow before God's messenger.—A miracle.—A miracle.

Jeremiah
[Gently] Nay, brothers, shame me not by your praises. I have no part in what has befallen. A miracle has there doubtless been, but it has been wrought on me, not by me. I cursed God, and he has blessed me; I fled

from him, and he has found me. None can escape his love, nor can anyone overcome his power. He has vanquished me, my brothers; and nothing is sweeter than to be vanquished by God.

The Elder
[Ecstatically] Jeremiah, Jeremiah, may God do by all of us even as he has done by you.

Jeremiah
Alas, that I knew not the Lord till so late! Alas, that I found you so late, my brothers! Dark lies the city, and dark our fate; but wonderful is life, holy the world wherein we dwell. O earth which I have despised, be gentle to me as I kneel; God, whom but now I renounced, be gracious to my prayer!
[He kneels]

I thank thee, O Lord, for thy gentleness toward me,

When I, froward and fierce, did thy service abjure.

For that thou whom I cursed didst with blessings reward me,

My heart will be grateful while life doth endure.

In life I will praise thee, in death I will praise.

With the bread of thy word thou dost nourish my days.

Let me bless thee for filling my soul with thy breath,

With that spirit of love which is stronger than death.

Let me bless thee for this, that harshly thou dravest

Me forth from thy face; that sorrow thou gavest

To me and to others. Nay, sorrow I bless,

For when men keep aloof, lo, the touch of distress

Makes them know they are kin. But the sorrows God sendeth

Are the firstfruits of storm, which in sunshine oft endeth.

I bless thee then, God, on life's journey the guide,

Whom all seek to escape, but from whom none can hide,

For the lowliest ever thy grace can best win,

And the sinner thy love, yea, because of his sin!

Blessed the man who can lose self in God!

Blessed the man who is chosen of God!

Blessed the heaven, in music ensphered,

Blessed the world, as thy mirror endeared!

Blest the stars which shine peacefully, far above strife,
Blest the quiet of death—blest the turmoil of life!

Baruch

[Throwing himself on his knees before Jeremiah] Jeremiah, my master, Jeremiah! Let not thy word shine upon us alone. Many are waiting in the marketplace, their souls full of fear. Give courage to the despairing. Fill the thirsty with the waters of life.

The Elder

Yea, strengthen the knees of the tottering. Console the afflicted!

Voices

Go forth to our brothers.—To them, as to us, bring solace.—Give them the message.—The promise.

Jeremiah

[Rising] So be it, brothers, lead me to them. I have been comforted of God, and now will I comfort others. Let us go forth, that we may build again the temple in the hearts of the hopeless, may build there the everlasting Jerusalem. [He strides out through the door]

The Others

[Surrounding him, some leading the way, while all the voices mingle in exaltation] Jerusalem.—Jerusalem the undying.—Prophesy!—On, God's master-builder.—Jerusalem endureth for ever!

THE EVERLASTING ROAD

SCENE NINE

For I know the thoughts that I think toward you, saith the Lord, thoughts of peace, and not of evil, to give you an expected end. Then shall ye call upon me, and I will hearken unto you. And ye shall seek me, and find me, when ye shall search for me with all your heart. And I will be found of you, saith the Lord: and I will turn away your captivity. Jeremiah XXIX, 11–14.

SCENE NINE

The great square in front of the temple, as in the first scene, save that now everywhere signs of the sack are visible.

In the square we see a medley of hand-carts laden with household goods, of packhorses and other beasts of burden, and of wagons. Men and women, preparing for the exodus, are busied among these. New groups continually flock into the square from the surrounding streets, and the noise of conversation grows ever louder. The women and children, together with the men too old for work, sit apart on the steps. Chaldean warriors, fully armed, stride masterfully through the crowd, making way for themselves with their spears.

The moon shines fitfully. Gradually the dawn reddens in the east.

Voices
This is our meeting place.—How many of us are here?—Keep together, sons of Reuben.—How dark it is.—This is the best place, so that we can lead the way.

Other Voices
Don't push.—This is our place.—Our mules have been standing here since evening.—The place is ours.—The sons of Reuben always want to be first.

An Elder
Do not quarrel, children. Let Reuben lead the way, for such is the law.

Voices
There is no longer any law.—The scriptures are burned.—Who are you to order us about?—It is the priests' commandment.—There are no priests left; they have all been put to the sword.—Hananiah escaped the slaughter.—Nay, they made an end of him too.—We are leaderless.—Who shall give us the law?—Who will make the sacrifices for us in Babylon?—Who will interpret the scriptures?—All of the race of Aaron have been slain.—Woe unto us that are orphaned.—Had we but the ark and the roll of the law.—The roll of the law has been burned.—Nay, the word of God cannot be burned.—I tell you I saw it perish in the flames.—Alas, is the

law burned?—Impossible, how can God's word be burned?—Has not his house been burned; has not his altar been overthrown?—Did he not deliver over his holy city to destruction?—Yea, yea, he has made us the slaves of our enemies. He has broken the covenant.—Blaspheme not.—I fear him no longer.—We are leaderless; would that Moses could lead us as of old; would that there were still a judge among the people.—What has become of the king, him whom they blinded?—He has always been blind.—To him we owe these disasters.—Alas for the fate of Israel, the destruction of Jerusalem!

[A disorderly rout, laughing loudly, issues from the palace. The newcomers are the princes of Chaldea, with slaves bearing torches. The princes are drunk. In the midst of the brawling crowd we see the figure of a man whom the princes are buffeting and pushing one to another, so that he totters, and is continually in danger of falling]

The Chaldean Princes

Are you ready for a fresh attack on Nebuchadnezzar?—On, stormer of Babylon.—Pillar of Israel, take heed lest you fall.—He cannot dance like King David.—He cannot play the psaltery.—Enough of him, let us go back to our wine.—I would rather amuse myself with his wives.—Let him drink darkness while we drink wine.—Come away!

[Laughing and shouting, the princes return into the palace, leaving the man of whom they have been making sport swaying unsteadily as he stands at the top of the steps. The moon has pierced the clouds, and his shadow stretches across the stone flooring behind him. This gives him the appearance of a gigantic wraith. The crowd beneath is filled with astonishment and alarm]

Whispering Voices

Who is it?—Why have they cast him out from their board?—Why does he not speak?—Look how he raises his hands imploringly to heaven.—Who is he?—Don't go near him.—Yes, I will see who it is.

[Some of the bolder spirits have mounted the steps]

A Voice
[With a cry of recognition] Zedekiah!

The Crowd
The king.—The blinded king.—God's judgment.—Zedekiah.

Zedekiah
[Falteringly] Who calls me?

Voices
No one calls thee.—For thee there are naught but curses, and God's judgments.—Where are thy Egyptian friends?—Where is Zion?

Other Voices
Be silent!—He is the anointed of the Lord, blinded by our enemies.—Reverence the king.—Have pity on his sufferings.

The First Voices
Nay, he shall not sit among us.—Where are my children?—Give me back my children.—A curse on the man who has murdered Israel.—He is to blame for all.—Why should he live when better men have died?

Zedekiah
[To one who has taken his hand, to lead him] Who are these who rail against me? Are my foes those of mine own household?

The Guide
Lord, they are thy companions in misfortune.

Voices
Do not bring him down here, for his lot and ours shall not be mingled.—Let him sit apart.—God has punished him.—A curse lies upon him.—No longer shall he be king.—Of what use is a blind king?

Zedekiah
[Wellnigh weeping in his helplessness] Lead me forth. They have put out my eyes, and now they will take my crown. Hide me from my enemies.

A Woman

Rest here, Lord King. Lie down and rest.

[A couch is extemporized for Zedekiah at the foot of the steps. The inquisitive gather round]

The Elder

Keep away, keep away. Reverence the Lord's anointed. God has appointed him our leader.

Voices

How can a blind man lead us?—He cannot reign in Jerusalem, for Zion has fallen.—We are all slaves, and slaves need no leader.—Nay, we need a deliverer.—Were but Moses here to help us at this hour.—How can a man so afflicted give us help and consolation?—No one can help us.—See, the dawn comes. Let us make ready for the journey.—Alas the day!—As wanderers and exiles, we go leaderless into a far country. [Loud chanting is heard in the distance] Hark, the trumpet.—Alas the trumpet sounds.— The first signal for departure.—No, no, that is not a trumpet.—Cannot you hear singing, with cymbals and drums?—Our enemies are rejoicing.— O shame! O torment!

[The chanting draws nearer and nearer, until individual voices and the clashing of the cymbals can be clearly distinguished. At length a group of persons is seen advancing, and thronging exultantly round a tall figure]

A Voice

Look! They are of our own people.

Voices

Impossible.—They are rejoicing.—How could any son of Israel exult on this day of sorrow?—They must be drunken with wine.—Assuredly they are our brothers of Israel.—Who is it in their midst?—Look at that frenzied woman clashing the cymbals!

[The approaching singers, Jeremiah in the center, advance in the pale light of dawn. Some of them are in truth ecstatic and unsteady in their movements, as if drunken; but others are of sober mien]

Chanting Voices

Hosanna!—A prophecy.—Jerusalem endureth for ever!—Blessed our return home.—Blessed be the consoler, and blessed the comfort he brings.—Hosanna!—Jerusalem endureth for ever!

Voices from the Crowd

[In excitement] They are mad.—What has happened?—Hark how they shout Hosanna!—Who is the prophet?—What is his message?—Let him deliver it to us also.—Who shall bring us consolation?

A Voice

Look, is it not Jeremiah whom they surround?

Voices

Yes.—No.—His face was lowering, but this man's face is radiant.—Nay, it is he.—How changed he is.—A curse upon him who breathed curses.— How can sweetness come from the bitter?

Baruch

Hearken to the message of comfort, brothers. Feed your souls with the word of God, with the bread of life!

Voices

How can comfort be brought by this man accurst?—His words are like scorpions.—His message will choke us.—We have had enough of the prophets, for they have misled us one and all.—No, no, Jeremiah gave us true warning.—I tell you he will rub salt into our wounds.—Away, away, man without bowels of compassion!

Baruch

I beseech you to hear his message. He has uplifted our hearts, and will uplift yours likewise, brothers in God.

The Wounded Man

I testify for him, I testify for him! Fevered by my wounds I lay unable to move. His words have restored my strength. Lo, on me he hath wrought a miracle.

Voices

Who is this?—Listen to what he says.—He tells of a miracle, and a miracle is what we need.—I need comfort.—Naught but Zion's valleys will comfort me.—What comfort can he give?—Can he raise the dead; can he rebuild the temple?—Let us hear his message.

The Woman

Balaam! Balaam! Balaam! Hail, for that you who came to curse Israel have blessed us thrice.

Baruch

Master, look upon their discord. Make their hearts one, their spirits fruitful. Lift them from their mourning, lift their souls to God.

Jeremiah

[Leaving his companions and going to the top of the steps] Brothers, in the darkness I feel you to be near me, and know that your souls are filled with darkness. But why do you despair? Why do you lament?

Voices

Hearken to the blasphemer.—I warned you against him.—He mocks us.—He asks why we lament!—He rubs salt into our wounds.—Are we to rejoice on the day of our exodus?—Are we to forget the dead?—He laughs at our tears.—Silence, let us hear him.—Let us hear his message.

Jeremiah

Hearken, brothers, give ear unto my words. Is all lost, that you should lament? There still remains the precious gift of life.

A Voice

What a life!

Jeremiah

And I say unto you, who has life, has God also. Leave it to the dead to complain of those who have led them to the tomb. We, who survive, should continue to hope. Lament not, despair not, while breath remains; neither opening your mouths in revolt, nor closing your ears to words of consolation.

Voices

Words, only words, which avail nothing.—If you would lift up our hearts, lift up the walls of Jerusalem.—Rebuild the fortress of Zion.—Alas, he cannot see our distress, he cannot recognize our suffering.

Jeremiah

Brothers, I read your suffering like an open book, and the scroll of your pain lies unrolled before me. Natheless, brothers, I see a meaning in this pain and suffering; I see God therein. The hour is sent to us for trial. Let us meet the test.

Voices

Why should God try us?—Why should he visit us, his chosen people, with affliction?—Why should he make our burden so heavy?

Jeremiah

God sends us this trial that we may know him to be God. To those of other nations, few signs are given and little recognition is vouchsafed. They fancy themselves able to see the face of the Eternal in images of wood and stone. Our God, the God of our fathers, is a hidden God; and not until we are bathed in sorrow are we enabled to discern him. He chooses those only whom he has tried, and to none but the suffering does he give his love. Let us therefore rejoice at our trials, brothers, and let us love the suffering God sends. He has broken us with affliction, that he may sink the deeper into the freshly ploughed ground of our hearts, and that we may be ready for the scattering of his seed. He has weakened our bodies that he may strengthen our souls. Let us joyfully enter the smelting furnace of his will, that thereby we may be purified. Follow the example of your forefathers, and thankfully accept the scourgings of the Almighty!

Voices

Not our will but his.—A blessing on our trials.—I must learn to stifle my complaints.—True, our forefathers likewise were in bondage.

Jeremiah

Brothers, if we believe that we shall arise, already we have arisen. What should we be without faith? Not to us, as to other nations, has a country been given to which we may cling; a home, where we may tarry; rest, that our hearts may wax fat! Not for peace have we been the chosen among the nations. Wandering is our habitation, trouble our heritage, God our home. Do not for that reason covet your neighbor's goods; do not for that reason complain. Leave to others their happiness and their pride; leave to others an abiding place. For yourselves, people of suffering, gladly accept trial. Have faith, chosen of God, seeing that sorrow is your heritage. Because it is your eternal heritage, therefore are you chosen.

Voices

True is the word.—Sorrow is our heritage.—I will shoulder my burden.—I have faith in God's mercy. He will lead us now, as he led us out of Egypt.—God will deliver us, as he delivered our fathers.

Jeremiah

Arise, then, and cease repining. Take up your faith as a staff, and you will march bravely through these trials as you have marched for thousands of years. Happy are we to be vanquished, and happy to be driven from home; for we are vanquished, we are driven from home, by God's will. Happy are we to lose all, that we may find him; happy is our hard lot, gladsome our trial. Kings who mastered us have vanished like smoke; nations which enslaved us have been scattered and their seed has been destroyed; towns wherein we served as bondmen have been made desolate, and are now the home of the jackal; but Israel still lives, ever young, for sorrow is our buttress and overthrow is our strength. Through suffering we have endured the assaults of time; reverses have ever been our beginning; and out of the depths God has gathered us to his heart. Think of our former troubles, and how those troubles were met. Think of Egypt, the house of bondage, the first ordeal. Give praise to affliction, ye afflicted; give praise to trial, ye sorely tried; praise the name of God who, through tribulation, has chosen us for all eternity!

[A wave of enthusiasm answers his words. The confused medley of voices gradually gives place to rhythmical choruses]

Voices
Bondmen of Mizraim
Were our fathers,
Bridled and bitted
Were our fathers,
Israel's children.
Taskmasters cruel
Hasted our fathers,
Beat them with rods,
Scourged them with cords,
Afflicted our fathers
With manifold tasks.

Higher Voices
Ere long the darkness which encompassed us
Was pierced by Jehovah's compassionate gaze.
To save his people before it had perished,
God raised up a deliverer,
One of the house of Levi.
Moses came to our aid,
A man mighty of tongue,
A man mighty of hand.
He led us forth from the land of Egypt.
He freed us from the house of bondage.

Exultant Voices
Those who had numbered but seventy
When they entered the land of Egypt,
Went out from it numbering countless thousands,
Driving before them flocks and herds,
And bearing with them great possessions.

Before their faces went the pillar of cloud,
Before them went the pillar of fire,
And the angel of God went before the camp of Israel.
Such was the first exodus,
Such the beginning of happiness,
When God was bringing our fathers to the land of promise.

Jeremiah
But new tribulations awaited us,
Fresh trials;
Forbear not to recall the days of bitterness,
Forget not those days!

Voices
Pursuing us,
Came the army of Pharaoh,
Horses and chariots,
And a multitude of horsemen.
With vengeful clamor
Did they follow after.
The sea barred our passage;
Death pressed at our heels.

Higher Voices
Thereupon the Lord sent the strong east wind,
Dividing the waters that the sea might be dry land.
The waters were a wall unto us,
On our right hand, and on our left.
Thus went we into the midst of the sea
Upon the dry ground.

Exultant Voices
With the clashing of arms and the roaring of chariot wheels,
Our foes, thirsty for blood, followed after,
On the dry ground between the walls of the sea.
They shouted in their wrath as they thought to smite us.

But Moses stretched forth his hand over the sea,
And the waters returned, and covered the chariots and the horsemen,
And all the hosts of Pharaoh that came into the sea after them;
Thus did the Lord overthrow the Egyptians in the midst of the sea!

Deep Voices
Thus did the Lord deliver us out of danger,
And lead us forth from the land of bondage.
Thus wonderful was the beginning
Of our happy and unhappy wanderings!

Jeremiah
Again and again did he pour over us the bitterness of death and the waters of the cup of trial, that we might be healed for evermore. Bethink ye of the scorching days in the desert, of the forty years of privation ere we reached the promised land.

Voices
Parched were our throats,
Blistered our lips,
Athirst were we
And anhungered,
In that waterless and barren region.

Exultant Voices
Then Moses lifted up his hand,
And with his rod smote the rock twice.
Lo, the stone was riven in sunder,
The water gushed forth abundantly,
The congregation drank and their cattle,
And the wanderers laved their toilworn feet.

Higher Voices
When we were weary, the Lord gave us rest.
He sent cool breezes
To temper the burning heats of noontide.
Bitter springs did he sweeten for our sake.

The wind brought fat quails from the sea.
When our entrails were gnawed with hunger,
Lo, after the morning dews had risen,
There lay on the face of the wilderness
Manna, small and round, the bread of heaven.

Jeremiah

Albeit, never was it granted us to live in safety.
Continually did the Lord chastise us with his holy hand.
Ever and again did he renew the tribulations of his people.

Voices

The nations stood
Against us in arms;
Greed and envy
Closed the roads
Of our pilgrimage;
Cities shut their gates;
Spears gleamed,
Strewing our path with death.

Higher Voices

Then God forged us new weapons,
Making our hearts like sharp swords,
Giving us strength against thousands,
Victory over tens of thousands.

Exultant Voices

Trumpets blew, walls fell down;
Moab was overthrown, and Amalek.
With the sword we carved ways
Through the anger of the peoples and the times,
Until our hearts stood the test,
Until we reached the land of promise,
Canaan, where after labor we could rest.
Here was a home for the wanderers,

Now could we ungird our loins,
Doff our shoes, lay aside our staves.
These staves put forth green shoots,
Israel blossomed, and Zion arose.

All the Voices
Again and again have we been yoked to the plough,
Necks bowed; again and again enslaved:
But never has he failed to break our yoke,
To free us from captivity and exile:
From all our afflictions, all our privations,
Never has he failed to deliver us,
To summon us home at last,
To grant us a renewed flowering.

Jeremiah
Have no fear, have no fear, that the Lord will forsake us!
Mistrust him not, brothers, in days that are dark!
For when he debases us, when he afflicts us,
The suffering he sends is but sign of his love.
Then bow ye, my brothers, bend necks to the yoke,
Accept gladly the lot by Jehovah decreed.
Know, that sorrow but proves us, that trial uplifts us,
That affliction, though sore, brings us nearer to God.
Each pang that we feel is a step toward his kingdom,
Since the vanquished on earth are in heaven beloved.
Up brothers, march onward, march onward to God.

Voices
[Ecstatically] Yea, now let us begin our wanderings.—Lead us forth.—We
shall suffer, even as our fathers suffered. Exodus and never-ending
return.—Hasten, hasten, sunrise is at hand.—Let us march steadfastly
into slavery.—Now as ever, God will deliver us.—We will all go, not one
will stay behind.

Zedekiah
Alas, alas! Who will lead me? Leave me not behind! Who will carry me?

Jeremiah

Who calls?

Voices

Let him stay where he is.—He is chaff for the winnowing fan.—He is rejected of God. [To Jeremiah] Lead us, prophet.—You shall be our master. —Leave the outcast.

Jeremiah

No one is an outcast! Whoever calls for help must be heard, for all our sakes.

Voices

Not he.—He is the cause of our troubles.—He is the rejected of God.—He is one accurst!

Jeremiah

I, too, was rejected of God, and God has heard my prayer; I, likewise, was a man accurst, and God has blessed me. Who was it, crying in his distress? Let me bring him comfort, even as I was comforted.

Voices

'Tis the man lying on the steps.—God's wrath has smitten his pride.

Jeremiah

Why lies he alone there? Wherefore does he not join us?

Voices

Look, his stars are darkened.—No longer can he find his way, for he is blind.—They have put out his eyes.

Jeremiah

[Drawing near the recumbent figure with profound emotion] Zedekiah! Lord King!

Zedekiah

Is it thou, Jeremiah?

Jeremiah

It is I, Lord King. I am thy faithful servant, Jeremiah. [He kneels beside the king]

Zedekiah

Scorn me not! Drive me not from thee, as I drave thee from me! Thy words have burned me to ashes, man of might. Now leave me not alone in the hour of mine anguish. Be with me, as you swore before God when last we met.

Jeremiah

I am with thee, King Zedekiah.

Zedekiah

[Groping for him] Where art thou? I cannot find thee.

Jeremiah

I am at thy feet, thy servant and thy slave.

Zedekiah

[Trembling] Mock me not before the people, nor bow thyself in reverence to one abased. The oil wherewith I was anointed hath turned to blood upon my brow. My crown is dust.

Jeremiah

Thou hast become the king of sorrows, and never wert thou more kingly. Zedekiah, I stood upright before thee when I faced thee in thy strength, but I bow myself before thee now that God hath brought thee low. Anointed by suffering, lead us forth! Thou who now seest God only, who no longer seest the world, guide thy people. [He rises and faces the multitude]

Behold, behold,
Children of sorrow, children of God,

The Lord hath hearkened to your cry,
He hath sent you a leader!
One crowned with suffering,
One scorned of men!
Who is more fitted than he
To reign over those that are blessed by defeat?
God hath closed Zedekiah's eyes on earth
That he may better see the glories of heaven.
Brothers, has any son of the house of David
Been so fitted as he to be king of the sorrowful?

Zedekiah
Whither would you take me? What will become of me?

Jeremiah
Lift him up,
Him who has been abased,
Pay him all honor!
Harness the horses,
Make ready the litters,
Tenderly lift him,
Israel's guardian,
King over Zion.

[The king is lifted with all signs of respect, and is placed in a litter. A trumpet sounds in the distance. There is a red glow upon the walls as the day dawns. The sky has cleared. A tremor runs through the crowd at the sound of the trumpet]

Voices
The signal!—The first signal!—God summons us.—The day of our trial has dawned.—Soon the sun will shine over Jerusalem.—The exodus.—The exodus.—Exodus and return.—Jerusalem.—Jerusalem.

Jeremiah

[With confident mien, strides up the steps once more. The crowd has drawn back, and he stands alone at the top, looking taller than ever in his isolation]

Up, ye rejected,
Up, all ye vanquished,
Brisk for the journey!
Wanderers,
Chosen of God and the world,
Lift up your hearts!

[A surge of activity passes through the crowd. Jeremiah gazes out over the city]

On Jerusalem's pinnacles
Now for the last time
Look through your tears.
Carry with you the image
Of the home you so love.
Drink your fill of the towers,
Drink your fill of the walls,
Drink your fill of Jerusalem.

Voices

Yea, yea, ere we go
Let us drink our fill of Jerusalem.

Jeremiah

Bend down a last time,
Piously caressing
Your native earth

[He apostrophizes the earth]
Earth drenched with blood and tears,
Lo, I touch you
With loving hand.
The memory of this touch

Shall go with me,
Shall be an undying hunger.

[He addresses the people once more]
Unceasingly,
Wherever we wander,
Shall we be anhungered,
Shall we be athirst,
For Zion!

Voices
Unceasingly,
Wherever we wander,
Shall we be anhungered,
Shall we be athirst,
For Zion!

Jeremiah
Wanderers, chosen of God,
Filled with your hunger, your thirst,
Having now said your farewells,
Manfully turn to the journey.
Look forward, not backward.
Stay-at-homes
Have home;
Wanderers
Have the world!
God's are the ways
On which ye shall walk.
Made wise through suffering,
Wanderers, chosen of God,
On, through the world!

The People
Shall we ever see Jerusalem again?

Jeremiah

He who believes, looks always on Jerusalem.

The People

Who shall rebuild the city?

Jeremiah

The ardor of desire, the night of prison, and the suffering which brings counsel.

The People

Will it endure?

Jeremiah

Yea. Stones fall, but that which the soul builds in suffering, endureth for ever.

[There is a bustle among the crowd as all make ready for the start. The trumpet sounds again. It is now quite light. The crowd, eager to begin the exodus, greets the second blast of the trumpet with a shout of impatience]

[Raising his voice to dominate the tumult]
Wanderers, sufferers, march in the name
Of your forefather Jacob, who erstwhile with God,
Having wrestled the livelong night,
Strove till dawn for a blessing.
March on in the morning light
By a path like that which your forefathers trod,
When from Mizraim forth by Moses led
Toward the land of promise their way they sped.
Scatter your seeds, scatter your seeds,
In unknown lands,
Through numberless years.
Wander your wanderings, watered with tears.
On, people of God; for, wherever ye roam,
Your road leads through the world to eternity, home.

[The march begins in silence. At the head of the procession, the king is borne in a litter. In due order, tribe by tribe, the wanderers fall into line and move towards the gate. They gaze heavenward, singing as they march, so that the exodus has the solemnity of a religious procession. There is neither haste nor lagging, but a rhythmic movement forward. The files succeed one another in an endless train. An infinite on the march]

First Chorus of Wanderers

In strangers' houses now must we dwell,
Eating bread salted with tears.
By an enemy's hearth, with souls full of dread,
Must we sit upon stools of shame.
The weight of the years will lie heavy upon us
When, captives and bondmen, we must serve men of might.
But from exile escaping, from bondage redeemed,
To Jerusalem homing, to Zion returning,
Our spirits shall ever be free and at rest.

Second Chorus of Wanderers

Our drink must be drawn from distant waters;
Evil their taste, bitter in the mouth.
We must shelter from the sun beneath strange trees,
Their leaves breathing fear as they rustle in the wind.
But we shall win solace from the starry skies;
Dreams of home will comfort our nights;
Our souls will find continual refreshment
In the thought of Jerusalem.

Third Chorus of Wanderers

We shall journey by unfamiliar roads;
The wind will carry us afar, through many lands;
Weary shall we be, footsore and weary,
As the nations drive us from home after home.
Nowhere at all will they suffer us to take root,
Perpetual our pilgrimage through the changing world.

Yet happy shall we be, eternally vanquished;
Happy shall we be, chaff blown by the breeze;
Kindred to none, and by none made welcome;
For through the ages our path leads unerringly,
To the goal of our desire,
Jerusalem!

[A few Chaldeans, among them a captain, have come out from the palace. Some of them are half drunk. Their voices sound shrill in contrast with the chanting of the wanderers]

The Captain

The dogs are mutinous. They murmur against their fate. Beat them with rods if they refuse to go.

A Chaldean

Look, Captain, they have not waited for an order. There is no sign of mutiny.

The Captain

If they complain, strike them on the mouth.

The Chaldean

Captain, they are not complaining.

Another Chaldean

Watch them marching. They stride along like conquerors. Their eyes flash with joy.

The Chaldeans

What people are these?—Have they not been vanquished?—Can anyone have spread among them false tidings of liberation?—What are they chanting?—A strange people.—No one can understand them, whether in their dejection or in their exultation.—Their very gentleness is a danger, for it has a strength of its own.—This resembles rather the triumphal entry of a king, than the exodus of an enslaved people.—Saw the world ever such a nation?

236

Fourth Chorus of Wanderers
[Here Jeremiah inconspicuously joins his tribe]
Through ages we wander, we march through the nations,
The tale of our sufferings ever renewed;
Aeon after aeon eternally vanquished,
Thralls at the hearths where in passing we rest.
But the cities wither, and the nations
Shoot into darkness like wandering stars.
The oppressors who scourged us with many whips
Have become a hissing and a byword among the generations.
Whereas we march onward, march onward, march onward,
Drawing strength from within, eternity from earth,
And God from pains and tribulations.

The Chaldean Captain
Verily madness has seized them. We are the victors, they the defeated
and the disgraced. Why, then, do they not complain?

A Chaldean
An invisible force must sustain them.

Another Chaldean
True, they believe in the invisible. That is the mystery of their faith.

The Captain
How is it possible to see the invisible, or to believe in what cannot be
seen? They must have secret arts, like those of our astrologers and
soothsayers. It would be well to learn their mysteries.

The Chaldean
These mysteries cannot be taught; the secret lies in faith. What sustains
them, they say, is their faith in the invisible God.

Fifth Chorus of Wanderers
We wander adown the road of suffering,

Through our trials we are purified,
Everlastingly vanquished, and everlastingly overthrown,
For ever enslaved, for ever enfranchised,
Unceasingly broken and unceasingly renewed,
The mock and the sport of all nations on earth.
We wander through the eternities,
A remnant, a remnant,
And yet numberless.
We march onward to God,
To God who is the beginning and the end,
To God who is our home.

The Chaldean

See how they are walking to meet the sun. His light shines on their foreheads, and they themselves shine with the strength of the sun. Mighty must their God be.

The Captain

Their God? Have we not broken down his altars? Have we not conquered him?

The Chaldean

Who can conquer the invisible? Men we can slay, but the God who lives in them we cannot slay. A nation can be controlled by force; its spirit, never.

[For the third time the trumpet sounds. The sun has risen, shining on the exodus of the chosen people, beginning their march athwart the ages]

THE END

Printed in Great Britain
by Amazon